CW00520662

Polperro's Smuggling Story

JEREMY ROWETT JOHNS

POLPERRO HERITAGE PRESS

© Jeremy Rowett Johns 1994

First published 1994 by Toby Press

Second Edition
Published by the Polperro Heritage Press
Polperro Heritage Museum, Polperro, Cornwall

Printed by Polpentre Printers
Tredinnick, Duloe, Liskeard, Cornwall PL14 4PJ

ISBN 1 898266 01 8

Contents

Acknowledgements

The author is particularly grateful to the writer and historian James P. Derriman for his kind and valued assistance given over a number of years in connection with the subject of this book. He also wishes to thank the Royal Institution of Cornwall, the National Maritime Museum, the Public Record Office and Mrs Sheila de Burlet for permission to reproduce material in their possession.

Polperro's Smuggling Story was first published with the aid of a grant from the Sir Arthur Quiller Couch Memorial Fund.

Cover illustration by Sue Lord of Polperro

Illustrations

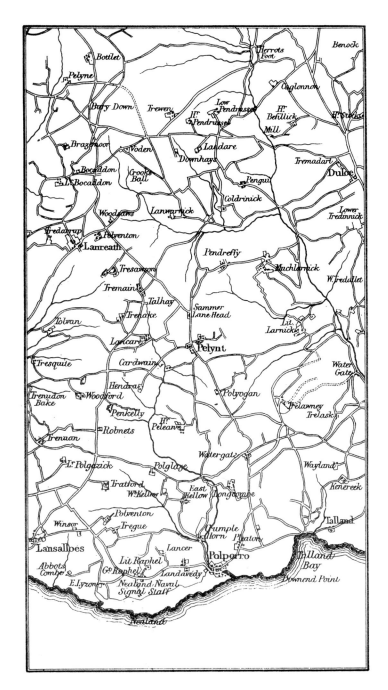

Situation of Polperro

PREFACE

Tales of smuggling at Polperro in times past are legendry. Generations of visitors to this picturesque Cornish fishing village have heard tell of the daring deeds of its earlier inhabitants, and there are many reminders still today of 'the trade' once carried on.

I first came across Polperro's smuggling stories several years ago in the course of a visit to learn more of my own ancestors who once lived there. It soon became clear that the Johns and Rowett families who lived in Polperro were, like the Quillers, Langmaids and so many others, actively involved in a smuggling trade that for a time at least earned small fortunes for some of the inhabitants.

Many of the published and anecdotal accounts of Polperro's smuggling activities are at variance with the evidence available from historical and official sources. Even Dr Jonathan Couch's excellent History Of Polperro, published in 1871, confuses some dates and events. Access to official maritime and Customs records as well as the letter-books and ledgers of the entrepreneurial Zephaniah Job has revealed much new information about the smuggling trade in Polperro during the late 18th and early 19th centuries. It has also been possible for an authenticated account of the period to be compiled for future readers and students of Polperro's smuggling story.

Where possible, I have relied entirely on primary source material. In some cases, the extracts quoted have had minor changes made to punctuation and spelling in order to avoid confusion.

J.R.J.

INTRODUCTION

'Our town was probably a stronghold of the contraband trade,' wrote Dr Jonathan Couch in *The History of Polperro*. 'All joined in it; the smith left his forge, the husbandman his plough; even women and children turned out to assist in the unlawful traffic, and received their share of the proceeds. That it was in any degree a dishonest pursuit never entered their minds; and if it did, they saw enough of the conduct of those above them to satisfy less unscrupulous minds that theirs was a venial offence. The gentry of the neighbourhood bought their brandy and lace; the excise and custom-house officers connived at unlawful acts, and profited by secret connection with the smugglers.'

Jonathan Couch's *History of Polperro* remains to this day a unique account of one small fishing village in Cornwall where circumstances combined to give rise to one of the most extraordinary episodes ever recorded in the area. Published shortly after his death at the age of 82 in 1870, it provides a vivid portrait of both the people and the smuggling activity once carried on there.

As well as practising medicine, Couch was a gifted naturalist whose observations contributed greatly to the knowledge and understanding of marine life in Britain. It is his description of Polperro's smuggling trade however, based largely on oral testimony gathered during his lifetime, that provides the setting for this book.

Cornwall's remoteness from the rest of the country and the daring of its hardy seafaring inhabitants gave rise to a smuggling trade that involved almost all who lived there, churchman, aristocrat and commoner, regardless of rank or status. The trade at Polperro reached its zenith during the wars with America and France between 1775 and 1815, bringing enormous wealth to many who lived there.

The conditions that led to the creation of Polperro's forty year period of prosperity were in part due to the wars that England was engaged in at that time.

High taxes on a wide range of luxury goods as well as basic commodities such as salt, imposed to finance the war effort, encouraged the movement of contraband goods. The rise of privateering activity against enemy shipping, encouraged by the Admiralty, provide further stimulation. But it was the influence of one man in particular, Zephaniah Job, that led to the establishment of one of the most organised and successful smuggling operations of all time.

This is the story of that man and the prosperity he brought to Polperro, evidence of which remains to this day.

Polperro (from an engraving by Henry Shore 1892)

CHAPTER ONE: FREE-TRADERS AND FORTUNE

Hidden away in a fold in the cliffs between Looe and Fowey on the south coast of Cornwall, Polperro's location at the seaward end of a narrow steep-sided creek made it an ideal haven for the smuggling trade in times past.

Like most other coastal communities in the 18th century, its population of nearly one thousand inhabitants depended as much on the sea for their livelihood as they did on the land around.[1] Generations of them had managed a meagre living from the sea despite the ever-present insecurity that such a way of life entailed.

Polperro's fishermen, like seafarers everywhere, were a hardy group of men resigned to their precarious existence at the mercy of wind and waves. In a good year when the pilchards arrived in abundance off the Cornish coast during the summer and autumn, there would be fish enough for all. If the catch was especially good there would even be sufficient left over for selling abroad: in 1795, for example, more than two million pilchards were exported to Italy from Polperro.[2] But if the fish failed to arrive, or storms sweeping up the Channel prevented the boats from putting to sea, they faced hardship and a bleak winter ahead.

A harvest of an altogether different kind, however, awaited those bold enough to gather it. Polperro mariners had long supplemented their living by bringing contraband goods ashore, considering the risks involved to be no greater than those they faced almost daily at sea. Tea, tobacco, brandy, gin, wine and port were all readily available abroad at considerably lower prices than they were in England where such goods attracted heavy duties and were often hard to obtain. By 1770 some 470,000 gallons of brandy and 350,000 pounds of tea were being smuggled into Cornwall every year at a cost of about £150,000 to the Exchequer.[3]

The outbreak of war with revolutionary France in 1793 led to further increases in taxes on such goods. Even salt attracted a tax of fifteen shillings per bushel, thirty or forty times the cost of the article![4] This was an extortionate amount to men and women in Polperro earning a shilling a day who depended on salt for preserving fish and pig meat for the winter. The fishing industry, already badly hit by the loss of its overseas markets because of the war, suffered severely. The fishermen were often unable to earn enough to buy salt to preserve pilchards for their own families; sometimes the fish were even dumped as manure on the fields. It is little wonder that smuggling became such a major industry in Cornwall during the French wars.

Smuggled goods were often landed at secluded coves along the coast on either side of Polperro: Parson's Cove below Lansallos in Lantivet Bay, Stinker Cove in Talland Bay, and others known only to the folk who frequented them. Once on the beach, the illicit goods would quickly disappear, hidden in caves or taken by well-trodden paths inland to secret hiding-places where the contraband could be safely stored before it was distributed.

Talland

Talland Bay was one such landing place, just east of Polperro. A lonely spot overlooking the sea where an ancient church stands alone within the sound of the waves on the shore below, Talland has long been the source of ghost stories and tales of evil spirits. If there were spirits to be found in the churchyard, they were almost certainly of an altogether different kind for it would have been an easy matter to store kegs there before they were taken inland or into Polperro itself, hidden in carts taking seaweed for manure to the fields.

The Reverend Richard Doidge, vicar of Talland during the early 18th century, was an eccentric clergyman reputed to have great skills as an exorcist. One contemporary account describes how he would often be seen in the churchyard 'at dead of night to the terror of passers-by, driving about the evil spirits; many of them were seen, in all sorts of shapes, flying and running before him, and he pursuing them with his whip in a most daring manner.'[5] The likelihood was, however, that the 'shapes' were in reality local smugglers engaged in their highly profitable nocturnal business. To what extent such activity was carried on with the knowledge or approval of the legendary Parson Doidge can only be guessed.

Often the Talland smugglers had difficulty getting their contraband cargo inland. Laden horses were liable to be searched. Waggons were noisy. An 18th century Polperro smuggling legend tells of the time of a local smallpox epidemic when the dead were buried at night. The landlord of the Halfway House Inn, 'Battling Billy', hit on the idea of conveying his kegs in a hearse, knowing no Revenue officer would stop a hearse. This ruse worked well until one night, everything went wrong. A cargo of brandy had been landed at Talland Bay which had to be moved by daylight, and the hearse would not hold it all. When Billy turned up with a second hearse his men, growing nervous, were ready to run away, but under the lash of his tongue they got the second consignment aboard. As the last keg was being loaded, the Preventive men came riding into Talland.

'If they shoot me dead, my body'll drive the load to Polperro,' swore Billy, leaping on the box; and lashing his horses, he drove like a madman, shots flying around him. Fishermen in Polperro that night heard the hearse rattling over the cobbled street, and opening their doors, were horrified to see that 'Battling Billy' had been shot through the neck so that his head hung over one shoulder, but his arm still lashed the maddened horses on until hearse, horses and corpse plunged over the quay into the harbour. Afterwards, the fishermen said they knew when the ghost of 'Battling Billy' was coming, and until he had passed they kept their doors shut and their backs to the window lest they should see him and suffer the death he brought in his wake.[6]

Ghosts or not, the coves and cliffs around Polperro were often frequented by folk engaged in running goods ashore under the cover of darkness, perhaps by moonlight. So prevalent was the trade that not even John Wesley's two visits to Polperro, the last in 1768, could persuade local Methodists to renounce their outlawed trade despite his preaching against it. On an earlier visit to Cornwall, Wesley recorded: 'An accursed thing among them: wellnigh one and all bought or sold uncustomed goods.'[7]

Zephaniah Job

To be successful, smuggling had to be properly organised. Ships had to be correctly loaded and unloaded, usually at night in winter with no lights. And to land a cargo of tubs in Lantivet Bay or Talland Bay in stormy weather would have been no easy task.[8] Before casks of liquor were taken aboard at Guernsey they would be slung with ropes so that they could be quickly and easily carried by tub-carriers or horses as soon as they were ashore. Sometimes the casks were strung together in case it became necessary to drop them in the sea with weights attached for recovery later. Horses and carts had to be hired from the farms and brought to the right place at the right time before daybreak. And arrangements had to be made for the watchers on shore to light fires to warn ships that Excise or Revenue men were in the area.

Smuggling was thus carried on as it was around the coast of Cornwall and elsewhere. But the arrival of a young man by the name of Zephaniah Job at Polperro sometime around 1770 was to provide the necessary organisational skill required to make smuggling there successful.

In due course Zephaniah Job became the main Polperro agent for the suppliers of the goods shipped over from the Channel Islands. He kept careful account of every transaction, collected the money and arranged payment, writing letters and instructing lawyers when necessary. So great was his influence on this trade, as the next chapter reveals, that Job became known as the 'Smugglers' Banker'.[9]

He helped a large number of Polperro people by managing their financial affairs, enabling them to save enough money to buy the freehold of their rented farms and houses. For many years Job was adviser, accountant and banker to the community. When the Polperro smugglers fell foul of the law, he hired lawyers in Liskeard and London, sending money to them while they were in prison. He was also banker and business manager for the local gentry. In due course he built up a considerable business which involved the ownership and management of several local farms and properties, and he saw that much of the profit from the smuggling trade he organised was ploughed back into the economy of Polperro.

Job was a prodigious letter writer. He kept copies of almost all his correspondence in a series of letter-books some of which, along with his ledgers and account books, survive to this day. These give a fascinating insight into the manner in which he conducted a thriving but unlawful business. They reveal how the Polperro smugglers regularly got their supplies from Guernsey on credit terms extending over several months, allowing them time to sell the goods. Job collected payments from the smugglers, acted as guarantor for them and forwarded the money to the Guernsey dealers, either directly or through a London agent.

Guernsey

The Channel Islands, exempt from taxation imposed by a British parliament, had become an important centre for the supply of a wide range of contraband goods into Britain during the 17th and 18th centuries. One estimate has put the annual revenue from Guernsey's smuggling trade at the time at over £40,000, more than the total value of the island's legitimate exports to England in the course of a year.[10] In spite of Britain's attempts to impose an effective customs administration there to suppress the trade, the islands continued to prosper as a base for smugglers until the early 1800's. Guernsey enjoyed particular advantage as a distribution centre because of its geographical position, deep sheltered anchorage and freedom from import duties.

The Guernsey merchants at St Peter Port imported large quantities of gin (Geneva) from Rotterdam, brandy from France and Spain, rum from the West Indies, tobacco from Virginia and tea via the powerful East India Company from China. By the end of the eighteenth century an estimated four to five million gallons of spirits were imported annually into the island, almost all for sale to English wholesalers and smugglers.[11] Because of the proximity of Cornwall the trade there was particularly active, although it had been in existence long before the goods concerned became contraband. Guernsey merchants did not consider it illegal since they merely supplied the smugglers; they did not do the smuggling.

Of the many Guernsey merchant houses that supplied the Polperro smugglers, that of Jersey and De Lisle (later Peter De Lisle & Sons) features often in the many surviving letters written by Zephaniah Job from Polperro.

The correspondence reveals considerable detail of the trade at that time, not least the difficulty obtaining payment for goods and the effect of any seizure of them. All orders were passed on by Job on the understanding that they would be paid for even if the cargo was lost or seized in transit by the Revenue cutters that patrolled the Channel.

In January, 1788, Job wrote to Messrs Jersey and De Lisle:

'In these very precarious times I don't know who to recommend, for those who are fair and honest while they have good success too often make shifts and are unwilling to pay when they meet with losses. On the whole I would recommend not to trust any (unless a few friends who you will know) too far; these should have no more goods until they pay off. Thomas Rowett I am sorry to say is a ruined man. No man has been more unfortunate. Five or six vessels in which he had goods and held a share in some of them have been taken.'[12]

A few months later, he warned one of the Guernsey firms:

'People in your line ought to be very careful who they give credit to in these precarious times, though the people of this place have always paid their merchants for their goods.[13]

The following year, Job felt able to recommend to another of the Guernsey merchants, De Carteret & Co. (later Carteret Priaulx):

'Please also supply John Toms with such goods as he may want, and desire you will supply him on the very lowest terms as he is a good dealer and always pays his bills quickly.'[14]

In June 1795, Job wrote again to Carteret Priaulx, following the capture of three Polperro boats within sight of the Cornish coast:

'I am very sorry to say that all three vessels were seized on their passage over. Willcock, Pascho and Co. positively declare they were never within the limits of a port and were at least eight leagues off the land when they were taken. A small boat was in sight and they can get the Captain of it to certify the truth of their operations. I have therefore ordered Mr Robins, Attorney at Law at Liskeard, to enter a claim on their behalf. They desired me to ask if you will bear one half the expence with them to bring on the tryal - I believe it will be the quickest way for you to have the money.'[15]

Anti-smuggling legislation made boats over a certain size and construction liable to forfeiture if they were found hovering within eight leagues of the coast. Although such losses often made it difficult for Job to get the smugglers to pay for goods sent across the Channel, the St Peter Port merchants knew they could rely on him to settle their accounts. They could also depend upon his discretion. In May 1796 he wrote to John Lukis at Guernsey:

'I have no doubt of selling some cargoes on the terms you mention for ready money, and you may rely on my secrecy. I have just mentioned to one or two particular persons that I can procure them a cargo or two of goods at the current price at the time of shipping it, to allow 10 per cent for ready money and no abatement for loss; but have mentioned no name nor will I until the bargain is made and then I will bind to secrecy.'[16]

The discount for ready money - cash on delivery - was an added incentive for prompt payment. From time to time one of the Guernsey merchants would arrive in Polperro in person to collect money. Job recorded payment in 1778 of fifty guineas to 'Mr De Lisle at Polperro'[17] and in June 1787 he wrote to Nicholas Maingy & Brothers, one of Carteret Priaulx's chief rivals in Guernsey:

'I had yesterday the pleasure to see your Mr Thomas Maingy at Polperro...'[18]

Letter of Marque (1778)

Reproduced by kind permission of the National Maritime Museum

Privateering

Polperro's connection with Guernsey was not confined to smuggling. The island had also become an important base for privateers, armed vessels belonging to private owners that were authorised by the Admiralty to attack and seize enemy shipping. When war broke out in 1774 between England and her rebel colonies in America, privateering was once again permitted and Guernsey bought many vessels formerly employed as smugglers and fitted them out as privateers. But when France joined the war on the side of the American rebels in 1778 there was a rush of applications by both Channel Island and Cornish boat owners for the necessary licences (letters of marque) against French vessels in the hope of securing lucrative prizes. As with smuggling, the risks were great but the rewards were often greater still.

Privateering was regarded by many as little short of legalised piracy. Lord Nelson objected in 1804 that 'the conduct of all privateers is, as far as I have seen, so near piracy that I only wonder any civilised nation can allow it.'[19] Nevertheless, the success of the Cornish and Channel Island privateers was to make no small contribution to the war effort, and those owned by Polperro men played a significant part in this.

Privateering involved a great deal of administration and clerical work, however. Money had to be raised to fit out the vessels concerned, stores and weapons purchased and, most important of all, the letters of marque authorising capture of enemy shipping obtained from the Admiralty in London. When a prize was captured, it had to be legally condemned in a prize court - a complex and expensive process that usually required the appointment of an agent to deal with. It was for this, too, that Zephaniah Job's assistance was sought by those who embarked on such ventures.

When the Polperro privateers were at sea they often combined official business with their own personal and private enterprise. They collected cargoes of liquor and other goods from Guernsey and sold them again upon their return. The French government was well aware of the illicit trade and was only too happy to deprive the British government of revenue.

One effect of the wars with France and America was the opportunity they gave to the Cornish smugglers to pursue their trade almost unhindered since both naval men-of-war and Revenue cruisers were preoccupied with national defence.

Polperro Boats

Many of the Polperro vessels were fast sailing luggers, shallow draft boats able to operate close inshore. Built for speed and manoeuvrability, they often carried a large crew capable of quickly handling the sails and outrunning even the deep-keeled Revenue cutters patrolling the Channel coast. The men who manned them had been born to the sea, aided by their local knowledge of tides and currents and their boats well maintained in good repair. Some, like the *Swallow*, the *Brilliant* and the *Unity* enjoyed quite spectacular success while cruising against enemy vessels. Others, like the *Sedwell* and the *Lottery*, were to end their days condemned for smuggling, their hulls broken up and sold by order of the Customs. Originally the Polperro smuggling boats were built elsewhere but as profits from the trade increased a thriving shipbuilding business was established within the harbour itself. In 1797 James Henna applied to Job for the lease of a cove under the Peak rock at the entrance to the harbour to build a shipwright's yard.[20]

The *Swallow*'s remarkable story is the subject of a later chapter. Both it and a large three-masted lugger called the *Brilliant* were commanded by John Quiller, one of the most notorious of all the Polperro smugglers. Like many of the boats fitted out for privateering and smuggling, ownership of the *Brilliant* was divided among several shareholders including Zephaniah Job and John Quiller. Job kept detailed records of payments both made and received in connection with the vessel, including the following inventory drawn up in 1786:

Hull, Masts, Yards, Standing and Running Rigging
good as she came in from sea.
1 Large Mainsail
1 Great Foresail
1 Trysail
1 Main Topsail

1 Working Foresail to ye fore Mast
1 Maccarony foresail
2 Storme foresails
1 fore topsail
4 Jibbs
3 Mizzens
2 Cables almost new & 2 Ankers good
1 Copper Kettle
1 do. Teakettle
2 Brass Compasses
with sundry other stores belong to the said Luggar
Brilliant[21]

The list of equipment belonging to the *Brilliant* was probably drawn up by Job to send to those he invited to take a share in the lugger. In September 1786, for instance, Job wrote to one of his London agents, Paul Le Mesurier:

'If it is agreeable to you to take the lugger *Brilliant* in £400 as Mr Quiller offered her for that sum. We shall be glad of your answer next post. Mr [Kenneth] Banks may then hold 1/4 if he choose to so - but it is not convenient for us to keep any part. We have since had an offer for the lugger but waited to hear from you having given you the price..'[22]

By October of the same year, Job noted that he had sold to John Quiller and another Polperro smuggler, William Johns, 'my 1/4 proportion in the luggars *Swallow* and *Brilliant*' for £197..10s. By 1794, however, Quiller owned 1/8 of the *Brilliant* which was then sold for £2,000.[23]

Among the prizes taken by the *Brilliant* was the Spanish ship *La Tortola* which yielded a remarkable £8,800 for her owners, John Quiller, his sons William and John and Zephaniah Job.[24] Such prize money, more than most men at that time could hope to earn in a lifetime, made the risks involved in such ventures seem small by comparison.

The *Unity* was a large lugger armed with 12 guns and commanded by Richard Rowett. The Rowetts, like the Quillers, were a great sea-faring

Polperro family who featured often in the exploits of the period. The *Unity* is credited with having made 500 successful voyages as a smuggler until her eventual capture while lying at anchor in Plymouth Sound with 170 casks of spirit on board as well as large quantities of tobacco.[25]

Zephaniah Job owned or had shares in a number of other Polperro boats. Some, like the *Lively* and the *Happy Return,* were evidently engaged in smuggling and privateering while others appear to have been innocently employed in freighting trade.

Job's involvement in the smuggling trade at Polperro was a crucial factor in its success. Given the instinctive opportunism of the seafarers who lived there and the precarious nature of their way of life; given the long-standing connection with the Guernsey suppliers and the prospect of rewards almost as great as those from privateering, there is no doubt it was Job's commercial flair that turned an opportune smuggling trade into the highly profitable activity it was to become for so many.

CHAPTER TWO: THE SMUGGLERS' BANKER

Zephaniah Job's arrival at Polperro must have caused almost as much of a stir among the little community as John Wesley's earlier visit there in 1768 when the Methodist preacher recorded in his diary:

'The room over which we were to lodge being filled with pilchards and conger-eels, the perfume was too potent for me, so that I was not sorry when one of our friends invited me to lodge at her house. Soon after I began to preach heavy rain began; yet none went away till the whole service was ended.'[1]

Job was born in St Agnes on the north coast of Cornwall in 1749. From an early age he had displayed a flair for arithmetical calculation which, coupled with an ability to write, marked him out for a promising career in the mining industry that flourished in that part of Cornwall. Accordingly, he was educated and trained as a mining engineer with a view to becoming a mine captain. The young Zephaniah's ambition was suddenly cut short by an incident the circumstances of which remain shrouded in mystery, although Couch mentions 'he was, when a very young man, obliged to quit his home abruptly in consequence of some trouble he had brought upon himself in a fit of rage.'[2]

An isolated community like Polperro would have provided just the sanctuary he sought after fleeing from his home in St Agnes. In order to earn his keep, the impoverished fugitive at first offered his services as a tutor to any who cared to send their children to him.

John Clements's Exercise Book

One of Job's scholars was a boy named John Clements whose surviving exercise book dated 1775 gives a remarkable insight into the teaching methods

Division

Division is that By which we from
how many times or ago sum is contained
in a greater

Parts of division

1. The dividend is y sum is greatest
2. the Divisor is the sum by which we divide
3. The quotient y the sum Divisor
4. the remainder is always less than the Divisor

Proof division (over this
proportion as the Dividend) is to the
Divisor so so the quotient and remainder

What shall 72 Anker of Rum each 10 Gall
Cost at 4..9¾ the Gallon —

5..9¾
      13
2..8..1
28..7..6
      6
173..5..0 answer

Bought 42 Hundred of Tea at 16..15..9¾ the
Hundred sold it at 2..3 the pound What did I
Gain by the whole

42..10..15..9¾ the pound
1..5..7
      6
13..7..3..3
      4
33..9..4..0

answer 71..0..9 gain

1..5..9
2..3
4..6

11
1..5..9
12..7..6
12..12..0
58..4..0
5..29..4..6

Extract from John Clements' Exercise Book (1775)

he used.[3] His fascination for figures is evident from some of the arithmetical exercises he set his pupils:

How many barleycorns [one third of an inch] will
reach round the globe?
Answer: *4105728000 barleycorns.*

Others required the number of seconds in 38 solar years to be calculated; even the number of waggons that would stretch end to end the eight miles from Fowey to Looe 'allowing six yards for the standing of each waggon.'

John Clements's exercise book also reveals the extent to which Job adapted his instruction to reflect the needs of the families whose children he taught so that they could assist their parents in the trade they carried on. Calculations invariably involved quantities of brandy, rum, tea and tobacco, all commodities then passing through Polperro as contraband:

If 12 gallons of Brandy cost £4..10s, what shall 134 gallons
cost at that rate?

What shall 72 Ankers of Rum each 10 Gallons cost at 4s..9d
per gallon?

Bought 42 Hundred[weight] of Tea at £10..15s..9d per Hundred.
Sold it at 2s..3d per pound. What did I gain by the whole?

If 14s will buy 8lb of Tobacco, how much will £14..8s buy at
that rate?

Many of the exercises Job set his pupils provide an illuminating insight into life in Polperro at the time: A man's yearly income was given as £29..18s..9d; a sheep would cost 12s..9d, while brandy was 7s..6d a gallon and rum 4s..9d a gallon. In later years, between 1787 and 1808, Clements used some of the blank pages at the back of his school book to keep account of expenses in connection with the schooner *Polperro*. One or two such entries suggest that he, too, had joined the great fraternity of Polperro smugglers:

1797
John Clements, William Quiller to Nicholas Maingy and
Brothers December 2nd to 50 ankers at 30/-
£75..0..0

Steward and Merchant

Job's attempts to establish a school of his own did not meet with great success. But he soon learned there were many who preferred to make use of his talents in other ways; as accountant, general correspondent and adviser to their business affairs. His surviving account books, letter-books and ledgers bear ample testimony to the extent and volume of his business affairs.

In addition to being the agent and banker of the Polperro smugglers and privateers, Job also became a businessman in his own right. He acted as steward and adviser to several local landed gentry and clergy. The Carpenter family, who owned the manors of Lansallos and Raphiel, paid him an annual salary of six guineas. John Phillipps Carpenter, a prominent lawyer, was even supplied with smuggled liquor judging by Job's letter to him in July 1796:

'I have spoken to Mr Quiller to bring a keg of best cognac, rum and gin which he hath promised to get at the first opportunity. I shall also desire my correspondent in Guernsey to send the best that can be had in the island.'

Offering his congratulations to Carpenter on being appointed a Justice of the Peace, Job adds:

'I sincerely wish more of the independent landed country gentlemen, and less of the clergy, would grace the bench.'[4]

It is little wonder that magistrates were often reluctant to convict those who appeared before them on smuggling charges!

As well as managing their affairs and doing much of the work that would be done by a solicitor or banker today, Job supplied local landowners with lime from the kilns at Looe, owned the barges that carried it, sold oats and barley from the farms in the area and had a substantial interest in the timber trade. He also provided Polperro with coal for many years and took charge of the pilchard export trade between Polperro and Italy until Napoleon's navy put a stop to it.

Even Job's meticulous accounts balance to within half a penny. Except for Sundays, he worked every day of the year and, as his exquisitely written letter-books show, his quill pen was not even laid down on Christmas Day in 1786! Every letter he wrote was carefully copied by hand, demonstrating just how prolific a correspondent he was. According to Jonathan Couch, he was instrumental in getting a daily postal service established between Polperro and the district post office at Liskeard.

But it was Job's stewardship to the Reverend Sir Harry Trelawny, the greatest landowner in the neighbourhood, that was to become by far the most prestigious role for the erstwhile refugee from St Agnes.

Sir Harry Trelawny
Sir Harry Trelawny inherited his baronetcy and the family estate at Trelawne above Polperro in 1772 at the age of sixteen on the death of his father, then Governor of Jamaica. The young Sir Harry was more interested in religion than riches and was duly ordained as an Anglican vicar, leaving the management of his estates in Cornwall, as well as the care of his wife and family, in Job's hands. Early in 1786 Sir Harry invited Job to act as his steward and agent at Trelawne while he visited Paris. Job readily accepted the position, and so began a long-standing association that was to link one of the most eminent figures in the county with the smuggling trade.[5]

Sir Harry seems to have devoted himself to his religious activities at the expense of his other affairs, leaving Job in charge of the entire Trelawny family, paying their household bills, the school bills for the children, Sir Harry's taxes on hair powder and the window tax for the manor house. For much of the time Sir Harry was in debt to Job, often for substantial sums of money; in 1799 by as much as £5,433![6] Job's surviving ledgers record that early in his stewardship he had obtained a 'note of hand' [IOU] from Sir Harry for £500, security enough at a time when the law allowed a creditor to secure the arrest and confinement in a debtors' prison of anyone whose note of hand he held.

This hold over someone of Sir Harry Trelawny's position is an indication of the extraordinary influence Job was able to exert from his cottage in Polperro. His account books record several payments made by Sir Harry to the Polperro smuggler, John Quiller, including one of £10 in 1777 for spirits at various times and another of £8..8s in 1799 for spirits and liquor during that year;[7] evidence that the neighbouring gentry had few qualms about defrauding the Revenue by buying direct from the law-breakers. The following year, Quiller lent Sir Harry £1,300, but would not accept Sir Harry's signature on the bond unless counter-signed by Job - in spite of Sir Harry being a clergyman, a Justice of the Peace and a baronet![8]

Job and the Quillers
It is quite probable that Job's early association with John Quiller led to his eventual role as Polperro's 'Smugglers' Banker'.

Jonathan Couch, in his private memoirs, relates how John Quiller 'distinguished himself as Commander of a privateer in the American Revolutionary War; especially by the capture of a French ship carrying military stores to America.' According to Couch, Quiller's prize was taken from him by a King's ship but he subsequently managed to get possession of her, 'in which service he was much assisted by the late Mr Zephaniah Job, then a schoolmaster at Polperro. The circumstances proved to be the foundation of the fortune of Mr Job who afterwards opened a bank at Polperro...'[9]

This account is remarkably similar to one related by Couch in the published version of his *History of Polperro*, referred to in connection with the *Swallow* in the next chapter.

A buccaneering figure and father of ten children, John Quiller's exploits as a smuggler and the owner and commander of several privateering vessels earned him considerable wealth and notoriety. Among his early successes was the capture of no less than four French vessels in the space of a few weeks while in command of the *Swallow* in 1782. The sale of all four, together with their cargo, was advertised by Job in the Sherborne & Yeovil Mercury on February 24, 1783:

FOR SALE, at the New Inn, in Polperro, on Monday the 3d day of March, 1783, at two o'clock in the afternoon, The Good Poleacre SAN LUIS DE BILBOA; Round sterned; burthen 120 tons, more or less, and is on account of her easy draught of water, swift sailing and excellent order and condition, a very desirable vessel; her cables, sails and rigging almost new; and being well found, may be sent to sea immediately, at little or no expence; now lying in the harbour at Fowey, and there to be delivered.

Immediately after the Sale of the San Luis de Bilboa, will be exposed to Sale,
The Good Chassemaree SAGE ALEXIS; Round sterned; burthen 50 tons, more or less; supposed to be two years old; is a remarkable strong vessel, with her masts, yards, sails, cables, anchors, standing and running rigging, as she came from sea; now lying at Polperro, and there to be delivered.

Immediately after the Sale of the Sage Alexis will be Sold,
The Good Chassemaree St. ANNE D'ARSON; Round sterned; burthen 30 tons, more or less; her masts, yards, sails, cables, anchors, standing and running rigging, were new with the vessel about nine months since; and is as complete a vessel of her burthen as any in England; now lying also at Polperro, and there to be delivered.

Immediately after the sale of the St. Anne D'Arson will be Sold,
The Good Schooner LE CHARDON; Round sterned; burthen 30 tons, more or less; being lately fitted out by the French for a privateer, has all her materials and sails in excellent order; now lying in the harbour at Polperro, and there to be delivered.

Immediately after the Sale of Le Chardon will be Sold,
About 38 tons of FRENCH YELLOW ROSIN, Of exceeding good quality, which will be put up in lots for the convenience of the purchasers.

N.B. The above vessels were taken from the French and Spaniards by the Swallow private ship of war, John Quiller Commander.

Samples of the rosin, and inventories of the vessels, may be had, and the vessels seen, by applying to Zephaniah Job, in Polperro.
Polperro, February 18, 1783.

The sale at the New Inn on the quay at Polperro must have attracted considerable attention in the area. Job's ledgers show that the *St. Anne D'Arson* was sold for £130, her cargo of wine having been previously sold at Guernsey for nearly £129.[10] The privateer *Le Chardon*, captured by the *Swallow* without a fight in September 1782,[11] fetched only £63, while the *El San Louis De Bilboa* and her cargo of wine, brandy and cloth was sold for £482, of which some £375 was left over after expenses had been paid for John Quiller to distribute among the *Swallow*'s owners and crew. The cargo of rosin from the *Le Sage Alexis,* much sought-after for soap and medicines, was sold for £554.

Even after Job had deducted his expenses for the various legal costs involved in claiming the *Swallow*'s prizes, Quiller would have been pleased with the sale of his privateering spoils in Polperro that afternoon.

The Three Brothers

John Quiller had three sons, Richard, William and John, all of whom were to play an active part in their father's smuggling and privateering activities. The firm of John Quiller and Sons is mentioned repeatedly among Job's records, and it is clear that Job himself had a share in their business.

As well as being one of the owners of both the *Swallow* and the *Brilliant,* John Quiller senior also owned a small lugger named the *Three Brothers* (after his sons?). He had bought the boat from the Customs who had probably seized it for smuggling, but early in 1785 found he was refused the necessary licence to take it to sea. Job took the matter up with his London agent, Peter Perchard, in May of that year:

'Mr Quiller is surprised to find the Lords of the Admiralty should refuse to grant a licence for the *Three Brothers* when the Act specifies such vessels shall have a licence on the Captain's giving sufficient Bond. Said vessel was sold by order of His Majesty's Customs and cannot proceed to sea without first taking out a licence, and if none can be had pray what could be the intention of such a sale or what is Mr Quiller to do with the vessel.'[12]

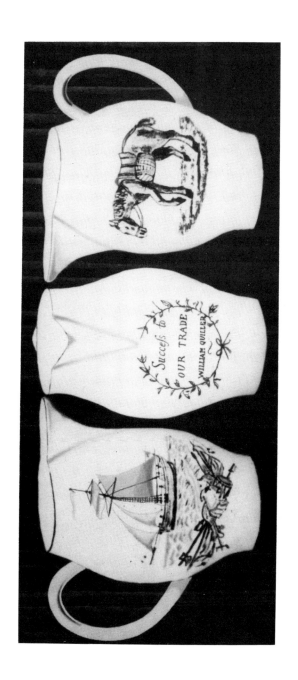

William Quiller's Smuggling Jug

The Customs Commissioners were obviously not convinced that the new owner of the *Three Brothers* had no connection with smuggling. In June, 1785, Job again wrote to his agent in London:

> 'It still appears very extraordinary to me that the Commissioners of His Majesty's Customs should order a vessel for sale which cannot be removed from her moorings. I beg leave to request once more on behalf of Mr Quiller that you'll please to apply to the Lords of the Admiralty through Philip Stevens Esq. their Secretary, to obtain a licence...'[13]

Quiller had incurred the displeasure or suspicion of the Customs who, as they were empowered to do, refused a licence for the *Three Brothers*. In due course, the vessel did put to sea, apparently to be lost ten years later. John Quiller had another boat of the same name built at a cost of £1,200, of which Job purchased a 1/16th share himself.

The eldest of the three Quiller brothers, Richard, married a Polperro girl in 1784 called Mary Toms (sister of the infamous Roger Toms mentioned in chapter 5) and named a brig he owned the *Richard and Mary*. There is a reference to the *Richard and Mary* in Job's accounts when he arranged insurance for the vessel and its cargo of pilchards on a voyage from Fowey to Venice, and it is quite likely that it too was also involved in smuggling.

Jonathan Couch's son, Thomas Quiller Couch, says in the introduction to his father's *History of Polperro* that the Quillers 'were especially a seafaring race, and suffered accordingly.' He tells the story of the key that hung on a beam in the home of the Quillers at Polperro, put there by Richard Quiller 'with strong injunctions that no one should take it off until his return (which never happened); and there, I believe, it still hangs.' Richard was in fact lost at sea in 1796, leaving Job with the task of settling his complex privateering and smuggling affairs.[14]

John Quiller was later killed during one of his voyages and two of his grandsons were both drowned in a gale with all their crew in 1812.[15]

Job and the Guernsey Merchants

Job's letter-books suggest that, apart from Carteret Priaulx's dealings with Charles Guy of Lansallos, the Guernsey merchants dealt almost exclusively with him when trading with the Polperro smugglers.

The smugglers themselves were given several months credit from the time the goods were shipped until payment for them was due. When there was difficulty collecting the money Job would bring his influence to bear; on one occasion in 1795 obtaining a signed undertaking from the owners of three vessels who had disputed a debt with the Guernsey dealer John Lukis:

> We are perfectly satisfied to pay the money to Mr Job, and it is our particular desire for him to receive the money for your goods for the future, as he hath been so many years in the practice, and whom we prefer to any other person whomsoever.
> Polperro 5th December 1795

> for the *Society*...................Richard Oliver
> John Oliver
> for the *Betsy*...................... William Barrett
> for the *Stamp & Go*...........John Willcock Jun.

That Job felt aggrieved by the attitude of the men concerned is clear from the contents of the accompanying letter to John Lukis :

> 'I felt a pleasure to find the people here in general expressing their sentiments entirely in my favour, assuring me they would pay their monies to none other than me, and that they never had any mistake for twenty years that I have transacted their business. Indeed I had every reason to expect from the assistance I have given them on all occasions whenever I have had it in my power to render service. From my intimate connection with the Magistrates in this neighbourhood I have prevailed on them not to grant search warrants and often saved them heavy fines when they have been prosecuted in the Exchequer. I should not have mentioned this but to show their ingratitude in mentioning my name to you in the manner they did. I had no idea they could

have done after the friendly manner in which they expressed themselves to me. One thing is plain. They have not the money to pay your bills for the present, although the money is safe and they will pay as soon as they can get it from their dealers, which they assure me will be in a few days.'[16]

It was Job who acted as the banker for such transactions. His role was to collect the payments from the smugglers on behalf of the Guernsey dealers and forward these, acting as banker for both parties.

A measure of the scale of this trade can be gleaned from Job's accounts for the period between 1778 and 1804. The sums collected by Job on behalf of just three of the Guernsey houses during those 25 years amount to nearly £100,000 alone; £30,500 credited to Messrs Jersey & De Lisle (later Peter De Lisle) between 1778-1789, a total of £23,000 credited to Carteret Priaulx & Co. between 1778-1799, and a staggering £42,755 to Nicholas Maingy & Brothers. On average the Polperro smugglers paid the Guernsey firms through Job nearly £6,000 a year between 1778 and 1799. There is no indication of the prices the goods were sold on for. Frank Perrycoste in his *Gleanings from the Records of Zephaniah Job of Polperro* suggests that if they were sold at even twice the price paid for them (allowing for the smugglers own expenses and a share of the profit), over a quarter of a million pounds sterling would have passed through Job's hands in a 22 year period:

'It is wonderful that during thirty years - and for how long previously? - such a volume of contraband was steadily poured into a small fishing village from a depot separated by a hundred miles of frequently very stormy seas.'[17]

Job does not appear to have had any difficulty in forwarding such large sums of money to Guernsey. Small sums were often sent across with one of the many Polperro boats that visited the island regularly. Larger amounts were either sent to one of the London agents Job dealt with who would in turn remit the money to Guernsey. In January 1789, for example, Job wrote to one of the suppliers, Peter De Lisle & Sons, informing them that he would forward the sum of £250 to Bonamy Dobree & Co. in London:

'As no waggon comes nearer than Liskeard I shall send a messenger with the light cash and enter it as such. I have however been pretty fortunate of late in receiving more than a moiety in Bills and passable Money. I hope your vessel with b[randy] is arrived, the wind having been some time fair since my last respects.'[18]

Subsequently, Job wrote to Messrs Bonamy Dobree & Co. the following month informing them:

'By orders from Messrs. Peter De Lisle & Sons of Guernsey I forwarded a parcel directed for you containing one hundred and ten guineas per Russells Waggon from Liskeard yesterday entered as cash and paid carriage as such. Please to place the amount when sold to credit of Messrs Peter Mourant & Co. of that island and advise said Guernseyfriends thereof.'[19]

In due course, Job even issued his own banknotes, printed for him by Alderman Christopher Smith who owned one of the London merchant banks with whom he had dealings. At a time when paper money was only just beginning to be accepted in place of coin, he accepted English, French and American money, always observing the essential condition of banking - to have sufficient cash available to exchange for his own notes.

Job's letters on his clients' behalf show that dealings with the Guernsey merchants were not always cordial. In October 1785, for example, he wrote to Messrs De Carteret & Co. on behalf of John Quiller:

I have since seen your mark on the casks you sent us of the *Swallow* and trawler. I find the report of your casks being much smaller than those of other Houses to be true. They have been measured and are positively two quarts each cask less than Messrs Jersey & De Lisle's, Mr Lemarchant's and all other Houses in your island who sell goods to this neighbourhood.

Zephaniah Job Polperro £5 Note

I hope you have shipped of the Swallow lugger this voyage proper casks same as others otherwise I shall receive great blame from my friends in the North having assured them your casks was <u>so large</u> and the goods so <u>good quality</u> as from other houses in Guernsey. Indeed had I known that you made such casks (2 quarts less than others) I would not have recommended your House to get the displeasure of my friends on any consequence whatever.

Mr William Langmaid of this place desires you'll send him of the trawler such goods as Mr Oliver may call for on his account and that the casks are the same as from others. He will pay me his bill £20..16 in a day or two, his payment is always a certainty. I wish you may have sent proper casks of the *Swallow*.

> I remain Sincerely Sirs
> Your most ob. servant
> Zephaniah Job

In spite of such difficulties the Guernsey merchants would occasionally treat the smugglers. In 1800, for instance, Nicholas Maingy and Brothers allowed Job to spend £10.4s.6d 'to all your Dealers a treat at Christmas'. And in February 1802 the Maingy Brothers were again debited the sum of £9.18s.6d for a dinner for John Rowett and his ship's company at the New Inn in Polperro. There is a similar entry for the crew of the *Unity*.[20]

From time to time Job would send his Guernsey clients legs of mutton and beef; they would reciprocate with port wine and spirits. On other occasions he would write with a special request, as on October 31st, 1788, to Messrs Peter De Lisle & Sons:

> 'I shall esteem it a particular favour that you'll procure and send me one anker Sherry and one anker Port. Let be of <u>best quality</u>'.

Several years later, in May 1796, he wrote again to the same firm:

'I'll thank you to send me a dollop of good Bohay tea and a quarter of best Grey Coffee for a particular friend.'[21]

Just who the coffee was intended for is not revealed, but a few months later in November Job mentions in the course of a letter to the Devon magistrate John Phillipps Carpenter:

'the coffee shall be sent by the first safe hand...'[22]

Job's connections extended to all levels of society. His letters reveal only a glimpse of the relationship he established with magistrates, lawyers, clerics and landed gentry, many of whom were quite willing to receive goods that had been smuggled into the country. As a result, he was able to exercise considerable influence when any of the Polperro smugglers fell foul of the law, often obtaining acquittals and even pardons for those who had the misfortune to be brought to justice.

CHAPTER THREE: THE SWALLOW'S TALE

Of all the Polperro vessels with which Zephaniah Job was connected, none occupied more of his time than the *Swallow*. Indeed, it was the *Swallow*'s capture of a French merchant ship and her cargo of military stores bound for North America in 1781 that laid the foundation for his eventual wealth.

A big three-masted lugger of eighty tons, armed with up to 12 guns, the *Swallow* was originally fitted out as a privateer in Guernsey following the outbreak of war between England and France in 1778. Two years later, having seized or shared in the taking of nearly a dozen prizes, the *Swallow* was based at Looe where she was owned by a group of Polperro men headed by John Quiller.

More than a dozen pages of Job's ledger covering the period between 1778 and 1786 are devoted to the *Swallow*'s accounts from early in 1781 when she was refitted at a cost of over £1,500, including:

> *12 guns and Shott - £60.3s*
> *12 carriages and blocks, etc. - £23.14s[1]*

Evidently intending to combine privateering with smuggling, the *Swallow* set out in July under the command of Thomas Effard for Lisbon where she planned to take on board a cargo of best Bohea tea, port wine and other goods that it was hoped would make a handsome profit for her owners who included Effard, Job, John Quiller and his smuggling associate, William Johns.

The *Rusee* Incident
During the voyage in the summer of 1781 the *Swallow* came across a French vessel called *Le Rusee* off the north west coast of Spain. The *Rusee*

had been dismasted in a storm and was heading for the port of Corunna when the *Swallow* gave chase and eventually closed with her disabled but better-armed quarry. For over an hour both ships attempted to outmanoeuvre one another, exchanging several broadsides in the process until finally the French captain surrendered.[2]

On boarding their prize, the *Swallow*'s crew found the *Rusee* laden with military stores, tea, cloth, silks and other goods intended for the rebel colonists in North America. Aware he had captured a valuable cargo as well as a crew that outnumbered his own the *Swallow*'s commander, Thomas Effard, decided to head straight for Plymouth after putting nearly half his crew aboard the prize. Two days later, however, they were joined by a large 18-gun Liverpool privateer, the *Harlequin*, which offered to escort the *Swallow* and her prize to a British port in return for a twenty per cent share of the prize money. Effard knew he was in no position to refuse such an offer from the *Harlequin*'s captain, Joseph Fayrer, and reluctantly agreed to 'protection.'

The *Swallow*'s commander gave evidence at the subsequent prize court hearing that after four days in convoy together 'the *Harlequin* made a signal for the *Swallow* to come alongside which she accordingly did, at which instant the *Harlequin* ran out all her guns and Captain Fayrer himself gave orders to fire at the *Swallow* forthwith if he, Thomas Effard, did not instantly come aboard with his commissions.' When Effard complied, Fayrer seized the *Swallow*'s papers, including her commission to seize French vessels, claiming they were not valid because the *Swallow* was a smuggler. After a brief confinement in the hold under armed guard, Effard was returned to his vessel along with eleven of the *Harlequin*'s crew, while most of the *Swallow*'s crew were taken aboard the Liverpool privateer along with the French crewmen.[3]

All three vessels sailed for Cork in Ireland where the *Rusee* was left in the hands of a small prize crew of *Harlequin* men pending the outcome of the claims to her as a prize of war. The *Swallow*, meanwhile, was taken on to Liverpool where the *Harlequin*'s agent began proceedings for a claim to the prize money due from the capture of the *Rusee*.

As soon as news of the *Swallow*'s seizure reached Polperro, Job went at once to Liverpool, taking with him sufficient money for Thomas Effard and his crew. He also appointed an agent who, he hoped, would arrange for the vessel's release while he travelled on to Cork. There, he later recorded, as agent for the *Swallow* 'I remained three months disputing the business with the proctor for the *Harlequin*, recovered the possession of the prize *Rusee* and myself brought her round to London and every day, actually on board, discharged the cargo and gave orders for the brokers to sell and pay the money into the hands of my agent Mr William De Jersey.'[4]

The sale of the prize yielded £3,100 while her cargo raised a further £5,824, earning a total of nearly £9,000 for the *Swallow*'s owners which Job asked his London agent to invest. But De Jersey died suddenly in November 1784 and his affairs were taken over by his son-in-law Thomas Bowerbank. Bowerbank at first disputed Job's claim to the proceeds of the *Rusee* and then delayed payment of the money to the *Swallow* owners for several more years. Job pursued the matter in a series of increasingly impatient letters to Bowerbank, the last in August 1788 ending: 'I am not the least afraid of your threats to protract the settlement of the business, being confident you will in the end pay dear for the unwarrantable delays which you have occasioned.'[5]

At long last in 1789, some eight years after the *Swallow* had first captured the *Rusee* and having resorted to litigation, Job received his £500 share of the proceeds.

While the complex legal matters that resulted from the *Swallow*'s seizure of the *Rusee* and her subsequent capture by the *Harlequin* were being dealt with by Job, the *Swallow* continued to earn substantial prize money for her owners from her privateering exploits, including the proceeds of the sale of the four captured vessels in Polperro in 1783 described in the previous chapter.

HMS *Beaver*
The wars with France and Spain came to an end early in 1783, and the *Swallow*, forced to abandon her lucrative privateering activity, returned to the smuggling trade under the command of William Johns, a 40-year-old Polperro mariner and associate of the Quillers.

AN ENGLISH SMUGGLER.

London Pub.d by Bothwell and Martin New Bond St. May 4. 1822.

Reproduced by kind permission of the National Maritime Museum

The *Swallow*'s luck ran out in April of that year as she lay, with a valuable cargo of tea, brandy and gin, becalmed at anchor off Lundy Island, a notorious haven for smugglers off the north coast of Devon. A party of the *Swallow*'s crew headed by Johns had gone ashore on the island, probably to make contact with the other smuggling gangs based there since Lundy had become a centre for such operations in the Bristol Channel, unaware that a naval man-of-war, *HMS Beaver*, was approaching from the north.[6]

The alarm was eventually given by one of the *Swallow*'s crew on shore and those still aboard the lugger, realising the threat posed by the naval vessel, cut the anchor cable and did everything possible to get under way despite the absence of any wind. The *Swallow*'s commander and the rest of the crew on Lundy hurriedly made their way down the steep cliff path to their boat and rowed out to rejoin their vessel as quickly as possible as night fell. Under the cover of darkness, the *Swallow*'s mate set off alone in the boat for Hartland Point on the mainland to alert Job while his fellow crewmen strove to put some distance between them and the man-of-war that had dropped anchor near the island.

HMS Beaver, a 14-gun sloop commanded by Captain Joseph Peyton, was on her way to Plymouth having returned from convoy duty between Appledore and Ireland when she encountered the *Swallow* off Lundy. Captain Peyton's log entry for Friday, April 18, 1783, records briefly:

Calm. At single anchor in Lundy Road ... Fired several guns to bring to the lugger. Hauled with our pinnace and boats, gave chase, rowed with the sweeps. At 4 came to an anchor. Manned and armed the boats and gave chase. At 6 the boats boarded her, Hartland Point SSE 3 or 4 miles, found her to be the Swallow from Guernsey loaded with Tea, Brandy and Gin belonging to Polperro. 11 came to an anchor in Lundy Road, brought off the smugglers anchor and cable from Lundy.[7]

At daybreak the following morning the *Swallow*'s crew were alarmed to find they were still in sight of the *Beaver*. Worse still, there was not a breath of wind to help them escape the heavily-armed sloop being hauled towards them by its crew in their boats. For much of the day the Polperro men pulled on the lugger's sweeps but, as Captain Peyton later reported to the Admiralty in London, 'by the great exertions and good conduct of the officers and men in rowing the ship, and with the assistance of the ship's boats, after about six hours chase we came up with her.'[8]

The *Swallow* had been caught within three miles of the Devon coast and boarded without a fight. She was brought back to Lundy under guard for the night before being ordered to sail under escort for Plymouth the next day where she was handed over to the Collector of Customs.

This time the *Swallow* had been caught in the very act of smuggling, with no papers to account for the cargo she carried. At the subsequent trial at Westminster Hall in London the following year, evidence was given by the prosecution that she was found with 119 bags containing 6,632 lbs of Bohea tea

'@ 3/6 p pound is Eleven hundred and sixty pounds and twelve shillings 1160..12..0. Two hundred and forty two Casks containing two thousand two hundred and twenty four Gallons Brandy at 5/0 p Gallon is five hundred and fifty six pounds 556..0..0. Ninety casks contg. eight hundred and twenty three Gallons Geneva at 5/0 p Gallon is Two hundred & five pounds & fifteen shillings 205..15..0.'[9]

Captain Peyton was a sick man at the time, and less than a month later asked to be relieved of his command, stating 'My ill state of health making me incapable of attending the duty of the sloop under my command, I must beg you will move the Right Honourable my Lords Commissioners of the Admiralty for leave to quit the sloop...'[10]

A year later, on May 21, 1784, he wrote to the First Secretary at the Admiralty:

'On the nineteenth of April 1783 (at which time I commanded His Majesties Sloop Beaver) I fell in with off the Island of Lundy and seized (having a Deputation) a Lugger called the *Swallow* William Johns Master laden with Tea and foreign spirits, on her perceiving the *Beaver* (the Lugger then being at Anchor under the Island) cut her cable and made every effort to escape. On my arrival at Plymouth I delivered the Lugger and Cargo to the Collector of His Majesties Customs at Plymouth to be Prosecuted, but the Owners having laid in a Claim to the Vessel and Cargo, a final Verdict was not given for the Crown until this Term in the Court of Exchequer.'[11]

Despite Job's strenuous efforts to secure the release of the *Swallow* and cargo from the Customs at Plymouth, it would appear that the claim entered on behalf of the vessel's owners was rejected when the case was eventually heard nearly a year later. Job devoted a whole page in his ledger for 1783 to the matter, headed 'disbursements on the Swallow when seized by Captain Peyton.'

Apr 20-22	*Expense at Plymouth with Mr Q[uiller]*	*1..18..5*
June 24	*Expense at Lundy Island etc*	*1..10..0*
July 3	*William Draper & Self: expense to London*	*8..19..6*
July 6	*Coach hire to Plymouth for 2 inside and 1 outside*	*5.. 2..6*
July 6	*Coach hire for Richard Barnes to Portsmouth*	*1.. 0..0*
July 6	*Expence at the Bell Inn, London;* *Coach hire up from Portsmouth and hire* *of the vessel: paid Mr Parkinson*	*9..17..1*
July 13	*To my coach hire and expense from* *London to Cornwall*	*5..15..6*
July 13	*Cash paid to Mr Parkinson for men's* *clothes and expense to London*	*28.. 2..9*
July 13 *July 13*	*Cash paid to Mr Budd on his return from London* *Cash paid to Richard Barnes on his* *return from London*	*3.. 3..0* *3.. 3..0*
July 13	*Cash paid to Messrs Donne & Cox:* *Security for the Crown*	*60.. 0..0*

July 13	*Mr Budd's note for cash advanced to him on Lundy*	2.. 2..0
July 13	*Cash to evidences: paid Mrs Hoskins*	3.. 3..0
	Cash to Mr Budd: paid Mr Tinny	2.. 0..0
Sept 9	*William Draper for his loss of time on the Trial*	3.. 0..0
Dec 5	*To expense for self and five witnesses*	
	on the Trial at Westminster	65.. 1..8

Altogether there are nearly forty entries relating to expenses incurred by Job in dealing with the *Swallow*'s seizure by the *Beaver*, amounting to more than £191.[12] This total was shared by the owners of the *Swallow* who, as well as John Quiller, included Mrs Susanna Hockins, Mr James Tinny and Mr Petherick Lukey, all of whom appear to have given evidence on behalf of their claim for the vessel and its valuable cargo. William Draper and Richard Barnes were both members of the *Swallow*'s crew, while Donne & Cox were the lawyers instructed by Job.

As a result of the verdict, Captain Peyton asked the Admiralty to consider awarding a share of the proceeds, estimated by the court to amount to some £2,322, to the officers and men of *HMS Beaver*:

'From the great exertions of the *Beaver*'s ship's company I must beg you will be pleased to lay the case before my Lords Commissioners of the Admiralty and hope their Lordships will think proper to direct His Majesties moiety to be given to the officers and men...'[13]

If the profits from smuggling were large, so too were the risks and losses. The loss of such a valuable cargo as that seized aboard the *Swallow* would have been a severe blow indeed to the lugger's owners, even to Zephaniah Job, at that time still patiently awaiting the proceeds from the capture of the *Rusee* in 1781.

Couch's account in *The History of Polperro* of a privateer that captured a 'Frenchman laden with materials of war' is in all probability a reference to the *Swallow*'s seizure of the *Rusee*. He relates how 'both the privateer and her capture were brought to the harbour of Cork' where they were detained by an English sloop-of-war. On learning of the detention of the prize, Job set out for Cork where he succeeded 'in re-obtaining the prize, which was forthwith taken to Plymouth. The prize was sold, and either as his share, or with it an additional reward for his services, Job recieved £500 which laid the foundation of his fortune.'

More likely, Couch's account is a conflation of the two incidents involving the *Swallow* already described. What is certain is that the episode marked a significant stage in Job's involvement with the Polperro smuggling fraternity.

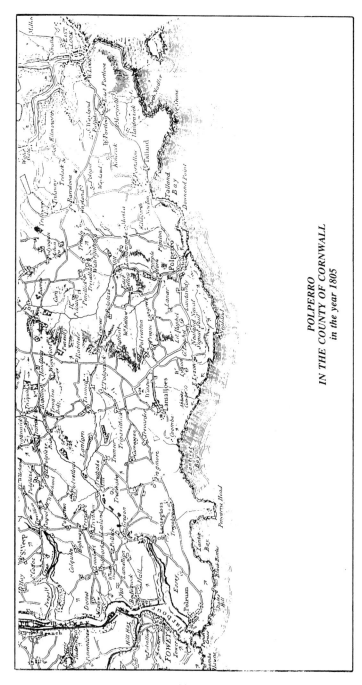

POLPERRO
IN THE COUNTY OF CORNWALL
in the year 1805

Map of Polperro Coast

38

CHAPTER FOUR: POLPERRO AND THE REVENUE MEN

The smuggling trade at Polperro flourished in the years between 1783 and 1793 when England was at peace with France and her neighbours. Many of those who had engaged in privateering during the years of conflict were quick to turn their attention to another equally profitable activity.

Surrounded on all sides to landward by hills overlooking steep-sided valleys and thickly-wooded slopes, Polperro's isolated position made it particularly difficult for the authorities to catch the smugglers in possession of contraband goods. Repeated attempts by Excise officers to seize such goods there following a tip-off were more often than not frustrated, despite the fact that a Customs Officer, Thomas Pinsent, had been resident there since 1766.[1]

The riding officers appointed to patrol the coast were too few and ill-equipped to carry out the work demanded by their masters in London, whose knowledge of the topography of Cornwall seemed scant. From time to time the Custom House in London circulated directives to the posts:

January 16, 1788

Gentlemen,
Having received undoubted Information that great quantities of Tobacco and Spirits are intended to be smuggled into the country from France, and the Islands of Guernsey and Alderney. We direct you to give notice to all Preventive officers at your Port, and also to the Commander of such of the Admiralty cruisers as may be stationed in the neighbourhood; and you are in solemn manner to excite all the officers under your survey to be particularly vigilant in the endeavours to intercept these attempts of the illicit Dealers so that the Revenue may not be defrauded in those articles to the alarming degree it has hitherto been; And you are to give notice to the said Officers that we are convinced

if they were to exert themselves both by day and by night in guarding the coast, such fraudulent practices could not be carried out in the shameful manner they now are; and although the Riding Officers may not always have it in their power to seize the goods from a considerable body of smugglers yet if such officers were to keep a watchful eye on their motions and were to communicate early information thereof to the Water Guard they may thereby render essential services to the Revenue.

Couch's *History of Polperro* tells of one occasion when the Custom House officers at Fowey learned that a run of goods had been landed in Polperro during the night. Several men from a Revenue cutter were ordered to walk from Fowey to Polperro to see what they could find. Coming down Landaviddy Lane leading into Polperro, they met a farm labourer who they suspected of knowing where the goods were hidden. Failing to get information from him, they threatened him with impressment into the Navy if he did not tell them. This was no idle threat, and the man was so frightened he told the Revenue men that a large number of kegs were stowed in a cellar on the quayside above Yellow Rock. He promised to mark the cellar with a chalk mark on the door. Some of the men remained at Landaviddy while others returned to Fowey for reinforcements. Hours later, the reinforcements arrived and crossed the wooden plank bridge over the river to the Talland side of the harbour. At this point, several Polperro men became aware of the danger to the cargo stored above Yellow Rock so they loaded a gun on New Quay Head and pointed it across the harbour. One man lit a taper and stood by the gun, obliging the Revenue men to return to Fowey for even more reinforcements, leaving guards posted by the cellar door. When they returned the following day and entered the cellar, however, they discovered that the smuggled goods had been removed by the back door.[2]

The Revenue Raiders

The incident related by Couch bears a striking similarity to one that actually took place on March 5th, 1794, when three Revenue officers armed with search warrants led a dawn raid on Polperro accompanied by a platoon of fourteen soldiers from the Yorkshire militia. They called first on Thomas

Pinsent, the resident Customs Officer, who led them to several cottages, including one overlooking the harbour belonging to Richard Rowett (probably the same Richard Rowett who commanded the smuggling and privateering lugger *Unity* mentioned earlier). The senior Revenue officer in the party was a welshman named David Llewyn, the Excise Supervisor at Bodmin, who described the raid on Rowett's house when giving evidence at the trial that followed the following year:[3]

'There was a cellar under the dwelling house, and in that cellar there was some liquor... a soldier went in through the window and opened the door which was locked. We then went in and took one of the casks and bored it with a gimlet and tasted the liquor and to the best of my recollection it was brandy.'

Altogether there were some 200 five gallon casks of spirit in the cellar, still with the rope slings used to carry them. The Revenue officers decided to move the haul to Thomas Pinsent's house nearby, but as they began to do so they were alarmed by the sound of gunfire coming from the harbour area. A large crowd had gathered on the quayside opposite the spot where the soldiers stood guarding Rowett's cellar. Several of the men were armed with sticks, clubs and muskets; even a ship's swivel-gun had been brought out while others shouted and swore at the Revenue men and soldiers attempting to move the casks. In a nearby street where the Polperro men were assembled, another swivel-gun had been drawn up aimed straight at the door of the cellar, its touch-hole primed with powder ready to fire.

One of the Revenue officers ordered the soldiers to fix bayonets and advance with him towards the swivel-guns. Almost at once they were surrounded by a menacing crowd, one of whom grabbed the officer's cutlass and threatened to kill him with it if he and his men did not leave the area. For several tense minutes the two sides confronted one another in the narrow street near the harbour. Shouts, curses and threats rang out as the mob tried to prevent the seizure of the tubs until finally the Revenue men, fearing for their safety, retreated to a nearby inn.

Several weeks later, the Revenue officers returned to Polperro with a force of more than one hundred soldiers, intending to arrest several of the men known to have been involved in the riot outside Richard Rowett's cellar. One of those named was John Langmaid, a 25-year-old Polperro fisherman who had been identified as having threatened Llewyn with a bayonet during the confrontation on the quayside. Although none of the wanted men could be found by the soldiers on this second visit to Polperro, Langmaid was eventually arrested and charged with unlawful assembly and armed assault on a King's Excise officer. He stood trial at the Old Bailey in London in October 1795.

Old Bailey Trial

At Langmaid's trial, David Llewyn, the Revenue officer who had led the raid on Polperro the previous year, described the scene as he and his men tried to move the tubs of brandy and gin to Thomas Pinsent's house:

> 'We were alarmed by the firing of several guns or swivels... towards the quay, out of sight. I was apprehensive that the mob was assembling and going to rescue the goods. I was insulted by several inhabitants. There was a large number that came at last with guns and clubs, large sticks and [Langmaid] had a bayonet when I first saw him. There were upwards of a hundred people in the street ... a great many of them armed.'

> 'The soldiers were in the act of removing the goods and the mob came upon them and said they should not carry them from thence. One of them went to the cellar door and shut the door ... and said he would be damned if we should move any of those goods from there, that we should be murdered if we attempted to do it. The soldiers were drawn up. Mr Pinsent requested me for God's sake not to let the soldiers fire for, says he, if you do we shall all be murdered. I told them that I did not come to molest them myself and requested that they would let me take the goods out of town. They said they would be damned if they would, that they would sooner lose their lives than their property, and if we did not go about our business that they would murder us, or words to that effect.'

Llewyn's testimony concluded by relating how Langmaid, armed with a bayonet in one hand and a musket in the other, 'came up pretty close to me and swore he would run me through if I did not desist. I thought my life was in danger.'[4]

John Langmaid was found guilty and, since assaulting a King's Revenue officer was a capital offence, sentenced to death by the court. He would have suffered the same fate as so many other smugglers arrested for similar offences had it not been for Zephaniah Job's personal intervention on his behalf.

Among those whose good offices Job sought was the lawyer, John Phillipps Carpenter, to whom he wrote after the trial:

'I find John Langmaid hath been condemned at the Old Bailey. I'm sorry to trouble you again on this disagreeable business, but at the pressing request of his wife I have to desire the favour of you to speak to the Recorder, Sir John William Rose, to report this cause so favourable as possible to the King, as a petition will be sent up by this post on his behalf to His Majesty, signed by several respectable people.'[5]

Job also sought the help of Charles Rashleigh, a wealthy businessman and landowner at St Austell, in pleading for Langmaid's life, evidently with some success for in March, 1796, he mentions in a letter to the Guernsey dealers Peter De Lisle & Sons:

'You have I dare say been informed 'ere this that John Langmaid is reprieved on condition of his serving on one of His Majesty's ships during the War. Nothing hath given me more satisfaction than to find my exertions on his behalf crowned with success - I attended the County meeting at Truro and with the assistance of Mr Rashleigh and several other Gentlemen prevailed with the Sheriff of the County R.A.Daniell Esq. to write a strong letter to the Duke of Portland to intercede with His Majesty to save his life, and which happily hath been complied with.'[6]

Just how long Langmaid served in the navy is not recorded, but convicted smugglers were invariably sentenced to a term of five years in the army or navy if the court decided they were fit to serve. Many preferred being sent to prison instead of to a man-of-war, where conditions were often easier and the chance of remission greater.

The outcome of Langmaid's trial seems to have increased the determination of both the Polperro smugglers and the Revenue men. Certainly the trade with Guernsey continued, in spite of several seizures by Revenue vessels at sea. In September, 1796, Job wrote again to Peter De Lisle & Sons explaining the difficulty he was experiencing collecting money from the Polperro men involved:

> '...Joseph Pearce is wretchedly poor indeed and John Rowett died insolvent. I think Reginald Barrett (who hath been one of the most unfortunate men in town in losing so many vessels and their cargoes) is still an honest man... I fully believe he will pay the balance of his account. Mr William Quiller will deliver you this letter who brings over <u>one or two hundred pounds in cash</u> to purchase part of his cargo.'

In June the following year the same William Quiller, of the *Three Brothers* fame, was in command of a fishing boat called the *Vigilant* when it was seized by the Revenue cutter *Constitution* and taken into Falmouth. William's father John, the *Vigilant*'s owner, at once asked Job to instruct lawyers at Falmouth to contest the seizure on the grounds that the vessel had no goods of any kind on board at the time.[7]

'If this rascal was not to be silenced he would ruin every smuggler in this place,' he adds, explaining that he had arranged for several farmers in the neighbourhood to testify that Coath was a liar. 'I hope these men will invalidate Coath's evidence and that Messrs Quiller and Oliver will get through this unpleasant business. Should credit be given to Coath's evidence Oliver & Co. would be fined heavy for the goods seized in a cellar - which I hope however they will not be able to prove was his property.'[8]

Exactly who Coath was or how he came to give evidence against the Polperro smugglers is not revealed, although Job's ledgers refer to someone named Coath employed as an agricultural labourer at the time. In any event, Job went to extraordinary lengths to discredit the man's evidence.

Gabriel Bray and the *Hind*

It was at this time that one Revenue vessel in particular came to be feared by the Polperro smugglers more than any other.

The *Hind*, one of the newest and largest cutters then in service, carrying 16 guns and a crew of 41 men, was stationed in the Channel between Portland and Lands End after the outbreak of war with France in 1793. Her commander, Lieutenant Gabriel Bray, had already acquired a reputation for the fearless and ruthless manner in which he had tackled the smugglers off the coast of Kent ten years earlier. On one occasion, while in command of the *Scourge* cutter in 1784, Captain Bray confronted 'a noted outlaw smuggler' by the name of Brown in the act of landing spirits on the beach near Deal. The ensuing fight was graphically described in the Whitehall Evening Post of May 1st:

> Captain Bray boarded him; and though Brown presented a blunderbuss, both of them not being half a distance from each other, the Captain was not daunted. One of his men seeing his brave master in this situation, with a cutlass cut Brown's cheek clean off. Bray seconded the stroke, and with his cutlass nearly severed his head from his body and put a period to this pirate's life.'

It was not long before he made his presence felt in Cornwall. The Revenue officials at Fowey enlisted Gabriel Bray's help in putting an end to the trade that was carried on so openly in Polperro. He certainly seems to have been more successful than the earlier raid led by David Llewyn for in September 1797, Job mentions in another letter to Nicholas Maingy & Brothers:

> 'I am sorry to say that [Richard Rowett] hath had 144 ankers of the lugger's cargo seized out of a cellar by Captain Bray's men

as he came overland and broke open the door of the cellar where the goods was...
You may rely on my constantly recommending all the good dealers to your House, and I have not the least doubt that you will do your share of business in this place - I expect to see your brother Nicholas here in a few days.'[9]

Only the previous month, Job had written to the Guernsey merchant John Lukis in London to let him know that the *Sedwell* had arrived safely, but 'had a very narrow escape of being taken by Captain Bray, who took a small boat belonging to Charles Hutton & Co.'[10]

Bray led another raid in April the following year after receiving a warning that a large number of casks of liquor were to be landed near Polperro and stored in a cellar belonging to William Minards, a local fisherman. Surprise was vital if he was to catch the smugglers with the goods, so Captain Bray ordered the *Hind*'s second officer, Hugh Pearce, to approach Polperro from the sea with two boatloads of armed crewmen while he travelled overland from Polruan.

On the way, Bray called at the rectory at Lansallos to obtain a search warrant from the Reverend Charles Kendall before arriving at Polperro where he met up with Pearce. Leaving the *Hind* crewmen to guard the cellar where the contraband goods were stored, he and his second officer went in search of a constable.

Unable to locate one, the two men returned to find a large crowd had gathered outside Minards' cellar including Richard Rowett, his cousin Benjamin and brother-in-law Reginald Barrett. Bray later gave evidence at Fowey that the three 'were <u>swearing</u> that neither Captain Bray, nor Mr Pearce, nor any Custom House Officer in England <u>if they had a thousand Warrants and as many Constables</u> should enter that cellar as they knew no Custom House Officer had a right to seize anything on shore'.[11]

Hugh Pearce's account of the episode vividly described the hostility faced by the Revenue officers that morning in Polperro:

Mess.rs Nicholas Maungy & Bro.rs — Polperro 1/.. Sept.r 1797.

Gentlemen

        Your esteemed favours of the 4, 5 & 25 Ult.o

were all handed to me yesterday, the two former p.r Richard
Rowett who arrived safe but are sorry to say he hath had
1/4 Ankers of the Luggers (are ....ped out of a ..llar by Cap.t
Br...gs. You to he came overland and Broke open the Door
... the ..llar where the goods was. the latter was handed to me Ben.n
Draper who received safe — the Venus ..tter is also arrived saf.

    You may rely on my constantly recommending all the
good dealers to your House, and I have not the least doubt but
that you will do your share of business in this place. I expect
to see your Brother Nicholas here in a few days — You'll .....y
the enclosed account of my receivings and remittances that
Mess.rs Quiller &c. have made two payments on acc.t of their
& John Marks goods the 29 July — they will pay the ......
so soon as the goods are run...d off. So far they have had
good luck. M.r Rear & that Bowden have promised to settle the
remainder of their & others bills of the 14 .pril as soon as the
Harvest is saved in when I shall not fail to remind them of
their promise — Ry.d Barrett Johns &c. told me they had
orders from you to ren.t their own bills since my letter to you
of the 16 June — I have received and remitted as under for your
account — Viz.t

		£		
Aug.t .. p.d John Johns &c. note of 29 May		100	..	..
29 p.d John Quiller&c. on acc.t of their bill of the 29 & July		390	..	..
Sept.r 13 p.d d.o		137.	5.	..
... p.one f..v.. of B.Y. & one of G..n .....l me		1.	14.	..
I have received one Jafe out of the two,				
June 30 Remitted to Perchard &c.a		63	..	..
July 17 d.o		100	..	..
Aug.t 28 To W.m Pearce Expence to the Owners of the Venus Cutter P.d p.t of M.r N. Maungy		2.	8.	2.
Sept.r 1 Remitted to Perchard &c.		398.	16.	..
14 To d.o to d.o		500	..	..

I have received 100 Dollars of M.r Quiller in part of the above
at 54/.. be pleased to say if I shall send them over or endeavour to pass
them here at that price.

    I remain very respectfully your mo. Hbl. Servant

Gentlemen

        Zephaniah Job.

Extract from Zephaniah Job's Letter-book (1797)

47

'In a short time great numbers of people assembled, <u>swearing</u> <u>they would cut our livers out</u> and others that they would <u>drive</u> <u>us into the water</u> and Benjamin Rowett repeatedly swore that Captain Bray nor me nor any other Custom House officer in England should enter that cellar, and that <u>he would be damned</u> if he did not <u>shoot</u> the first man who put a hand to the door in order to break it open.'

Pearce's evidence told how he found himself pressed against the wall of the cellar by the mob 'when Benjamin Rowett violently seized him by the collar and swore if he attempted the like again <u>he would beat his brains out</u>.'

Two members of the *Hind*'s crew, John Hawkins and Richard Verran, tried to stop the crowd entering the cellar but, according to Captain Bray, 'were beaten and dragged out again and the door locked, leaving some of the smugglers on the inside who they heard stowing the ankers of spirits.' Verran described how the door of the cellar was opened by the smugglers in order to carry off the liquor that was in it when he entered it with John Hawkins. He saw a number of casks of liquor piled on top of one another before he was seized by several men who 'collared him and beat him' and Richard Rowett 'tore his shirt from the neck about one foot down and thrust him out and locked the door.'[12]

When Gabriel Bray and his crew, aided by a detachment of Lancashire Militia, eventually succeeded in entering the cellar they found most of the kegs of spirits had disappeared.

The two Rowett cousins, Richard and Benjamin, together with Reginald Barrett and John Minards, the son of the owner of the cellar in question, were later arrested and charged with assaulting Captain Bray and his men.[13] The case came to court at Westminster the following year in June 1799, but for some unaccountable reason it was not proceeded with in spite of the overwhelming weight of evidence against the four defendants. Had Job intervened yet again on behalf of the Polperro smugglers? If so, it was to be one of the last occasions he was able to use his considerable influence and prevent justice from taking its course.

CHAPTER FIVE: THE LOTTERY'S LAST CHANCE

The year 1799 was a bad one for Polperro. On May 20th the Sherborne Mercury informed its readers in the 'Port News' column:

Arrived the *Lottery* smuggling cutter belonging to Polperro laden with spirits from Guernsey captured by the *Hind* cutter, Captain Bray.

Behind that brief announcement lay the tragic story of the *Lottery* of Polperro.

The day after Christmas in 1798, Ambrose Bowden set off at night with four men in command of the Custom House boat stationed at Cawsand near Plymouth having been alerted that a smuggling vessel called the *Lottery* was unloading a cargo of contraband spirits off Penlee Point nearby. Rowing quietly along the coast they eventually came across a large sloop lying at anchor about half a mile from the shore. In the moonlight, Bowden and his oarsmen were able to make out several smaller boats alongside the vessel, later identified as the *Lottery*, taking on casks.

What followed was graphically described in the testimony Ambrose Bowden was to give several weeks later concerning the events that night:

'When he [Bowden] got within about a hundred yards of the sloop, some person on board her whose voice he did not know, hailed the Custom House boat amd asked what boat it was - to which [Bowden] answered it was a King's boat - upon which some person on board called out and said: "Keep off, you buggers, or I will fire into you."

'On this, [Bowden] replied that his was a Revenue boat and they might fire if they dared. By this time the Custom House boat was within about twenty yards of the smuggling vessel. [Bowden] was standing up in his boat with the Revenue colours in his hand and was in the act of unfurling them when the smuggling vessel commenced firing at his boat with guns or blunderbusses. To the best of his recollection three times rather quickly, in the course of which Humphry Glinn, one of the boatmen, was killed.

'Seeing Glinn lying down with his head on his knees and his oar out of his hand [Bowden] called to him and asked him whether he was afraid, ordered him to get up to his oar and row on - not, at that instant perceiving Glinn was killed - upon which one of the other boatmen looked at him and said he was shot.

'[Bowden] took up a musket which lay in the boat and returned fire at the sloop several times, upon which the people on board either cut or slipped their cable and sailed away before the wind, at the same time continuing to fire over her stern at the Custom House boat. Unable to pursue the sloop, they returned to Cawsand Bay where [Bowden] went on board of His Majesty's Ship *Stag*. The Surgeon and Mate of that vessel examined the deceased when it appeared that the fore part of his scull was shot away and that he was quite dead.'[1]

A notice in the Sherborne Mercury, dated from the Custom House, London, January 22nd, 1799, announced:

'His Majesty, for the better discovering and bringing to justice the persons concerned in this felony and murder, is hereby pleased to promise His Most Gracious Pardon to any one or more of the said offenders (except the Master or Commander of the said sloop or cutter, and the person or persons who actually fired) who shall discover his or their accomplices, so that any one or more of them may be apprehended.'

As a further inducement for one of the crew of the *Lottery* to turn informer, notices were posted in ports along the coast between Plymouth and Falmouth announcing that the King's Customs Commissioners offered a reward of £200 to anyone 'who shall discover and apprehend, or cause and procure to be discovered and apprehended, any one or more of the said offenders...' The murder of one of their officers by smugglers provoked the authorities to such an extent that they were determined to pursue those involved and bring them to justice.

The *Lottery* Captured

The *Lottery* vanished for over five months, though it was later revealed she put into Polperro the day after the encounter that resulted in Glinn's murder to change some of her crew before returning to Guernsey.[2]

According to Jonathan Couch: 'The smugglers were alarmed at their act, and from the dogged manner in which the officers of justice pursued them, they saw but little chance of escape. They were kept continually in terror, and were afraid to sleep in their own houses without a watch, or to visit their families except with the utmost secrecy of movement. At the dead of night, or at mid-day, they were liable to have their houses surrounded by a troop of dragoons, who made stealthy descents upon the town. They were hidden for days in secret closets (of which each house had one or more), or wandered the country by night, and lay concealed during the day in the farmers' straw houses, where often the tramp of their pursuers was heard as they passed near their place of concealment.'[3]

The *Lottery* meanwhile continued to operate between Guernsey and Polperro despite the hunt for her crew. Among the Carteret Priaulx correspondence at Guernsey to this day is a letter from Charles Guy, landlord of the Ship inn at Polperro, dated April 1799:

Gentlemen
   You will please to ship on board the Lottery on Account of John Willcock 25 Ankers Brandy and 25 Gin
   I am Gentlemen Your Humble Servant
       Chas. Guy

A SHIP HAS BEEN SIGHTED
in this quarter
ENGAGING IN THE UNLAWFUL ACT OF

SMUGGLING

whosoever can lay information
leading to the capture of this ship
or its crew

will receive a reward of

£500

From His Majesty's Government

This 19th day of October 1782

Revenue Smuggling Poster (1782)

Charles Guy was, like Zephaniah Job, one of the agents acting on behalf of the Cornish smuggling syndicates who dealt with the Guernsey dealers.

On the afternoon of May 13th, 1799, the *Lottery* was sighted off Start Point making for the south coast of Devon by Gabriel Bray aboard the Revenue cutter *Hind*. As soon as the *Lottery* recognised the *Hind* she altered course to westward. A fast vessel of her type, the *Lottery* tacked away down Channel, zig-zagging close inshore and out again while aboard the Revenue cutter, Captain Bray doggedly followed in her wake. The chase continued through the night with the *Hind* staying close but never quite getting within gun range. When dawn broke the following morning the wind dropped, as it often does at first light, and both vessels lay becalmed five miles apart off the Lizard. The *Hind* fired a gun and hoisted the Revenue flag, at the same time sending two of her boats under the command of the mate, Hugh Pearce, to board the *Lottery*.

The *Lottery*'s crew meanwhile manned their sweeps in a desperate effort to escape their pursuers. As the Revenue boats drew closer, a gun was fired from her stern and a crewman warned them through a speaking trumpet to 'Keep off them boats, immediately!'

To make sure his reply was heard, Pearce rowed up to within a cable's length of the *Lottery* when he was again warned that if his boats did not keep off they would be fired upon and sunk. Standing up, Pearce shouted that it was the *Hind*'s boat and that he had orders to board their vessel which he knew to be the *Lottery*, and that he also knew the men aboard her. The smugglers replied that 'they didn't care a damn who the boat belonged to, or who were in it; that the vessel was not the *Lottery*, and unless the boats kept off they would fire into them and kill us all.'

Pearce knew perfectly well that the vessel was the *Lottery* although the name on her stern was covered with a piece of canvas. He made a last appeal to the smugglers to allow him to come alongside, promising to treat them well if they did. But the only reply was, if he attempted to board not one of the party would live to return. At the same time, one of the *Lottery*'s guns was run out on the quarter nearest the boats and two swivel guns were pointing from the beam. Seeing this, the *Hind*'s second officer decided to return to the cutter, intending instead to pull her up to the *Lottery.*

At that moment the wind suddenly got up and both vessels bgan to make sail as the boats were hoisted aboard the *Hind.* The Revenue cutter gradually closed on the *Lottery* whose crew began to jettison some of her cargo of tubs. By early afternoon, off Lands End, the *Hind* was close enough to bring her chase-guns to bear on the *Lottery.* Realising further resistance was useless, the smugglers lowered their sails and some of the crew tried to escape by rowing to the shore in their boat. Captain Bray at once dispatched a heavily-armed party in his two boats; one to take possession of the *Lottery,* and the other to pursue the smugglers' boat which was captured halfway to the shore with twelve men in it. A further five men were taken aboard the *Lottery* which was found to be carrying 716 casks of gin as well as tea and tobacco.[4]

Toms the Informer

As the Sherborne Mercury revealed on May 20th, the *Lottery* was brought into Plymouth by the *Hind* where her crew, with one exception, were placed in irons to await trial. The exception was a Polperro man called Roger Toms who, in order to gain a pardon for himself, agreed to give evidence against those of his fellow crewmen who had been directly concerned with the murder of Humphry Glinn.

Toms named another Polperro man, Thomas Potter, as having fired the fatal shot aboard the *Lottery* the previous December. Potter was not among the *Lottery* crew captured by the *Hind* and Captain Bray wasted no time on arrival at Plymouth rounding up a party of dragoons and setting off overland to Polperro, determined that on this occasion at least he would catch his man unawares. On arrival there at midnight, according to a report by the Collector of Customs at Plymouth, Bray 'found Potter at his house in bed, by good conduct obtained quiet admission into his dwelling and immediately brought him off to this place where he is lodged in the custody of the civil magistrate.'[5]

Potter was confined in the notorious 'Black Hole' dungeon in Fore Street, Devonport, for three days while he was formally charged with the murder of Humphry Glinn before being taken to Exeter gaol where he remained until July when he was escorted under guard to Newgate in London.[6]

Toms also named two of the other prisoners captured by the *Hind,* William Searle and Thomas Ventin, as having aided and abetted Potter in the murder of Glinn. Because of this, the magistrate allowed Toms to go free. The remaining fifteen members of the *Lottery*'s were prosecuted and convicted of smuggling. Five were further charged with 'firing a certain gun, or swivel, and directing certain other firearms, and obstructing certain officers in the service of the Customs.' All five stood trial at the Old Bailey, were found guilty and sentenced 'to hard labour upon the River Thames for two years.' Imprisonment in leaking, rat-infested prison hulks on the Thames was a harsh and very unpleasant experience indeed.

Roger Toms was a key prosecution witness in the case against Potter, Searle and Ventin. Although allowed to go free, he was made a member of the *Hind*'s crew for his own safety but after only two weeks he disappeared while ashore in Polruan just a few miles west of Polperro.

Couch tells the story in his *History of Polperro* of how several friends and accomplices of the unfortunate *Lottery* men, on learning that the Hind was anchored in the Fowey estuary, persuaded Toms's wife Martha to go to Polruan for a secret meeting with her husband, promising he would not be harmed. As Toms walked with his wife across the downs above Lantic Bay in the evening twilight 'three or four men sprung from behind a hedge, secured him, and carried him off to some place of concealment.'

Gabriel Bray also referred to the incident when giving evidence later that year, maintaining that Toms 'either absconded or was carried off by force by about twenty persons belonging to Polperro and was met by one of the *Hind*'s crew about a mile from Polruan.' Bray added he had been informed 'that the smugglers of Polperro have kept Roger Toms closely confined and chained either in a cave or in some other private place for the purpose of preventing his being brought forward as a witness on the part of the Crown.'[7] Without him, the case against Potter, Searle and Ventin could not proceed and the trial at the Old Bailey was postponed.

The authorities, meanwhile, were anxious to complete the case against all the men responsible for the murder of Humphry Glinn. Not only did they need to trace their leading witness, Roger Toms; they were also eager to arrest the other members of the *Lottery*'s crew still at large who had been aboard her at the time of Glinn's murder. Posters offering a reward for information were distributed and the Collector of Customs at Plymouth urged 'that the same may be published in the provincial newspapers of this neighbourhood for one month as the smugglers are in the habit of pulling down the advertisements that are posted in the most usual places of their residence.'[8] The Sherborne Mercury of November 4th 1799, published one of the most extraordinary notices of its kind ever issued by the Commissioners of Customs:

> "Whereas it has been humbly represented to the King that RICHARD OLIVER, the Younger, RICHARD BARRETT, the Younger, WILLIAM SWARTMAN, the Younger, PHILIP LIBBY, the Younger, THOMAS GEORGE, and ROGER TOMS, of Polperrow, in the County of Cornwall, mariners, and lately belonging to a smuggling vessel called the Lottery, stand charged upon oath with being concerned with the WILFUL MURDER of HUMPHREY GLINN, late a boatman belonging to the six-oared boat in the service of the Customs, stationed at Cawsand, on the 26th of December last, between the hours of ten and eleven at night, off Penlee Point, on the coast of Cornwall, by firing from on board the said vessel called the Lottery with muskets at the said boat,
>
> "His Majesty, for the better discovering and bringing to justice the above-named persons, is hereby pleased to promise his most gracious pardon to any one of the said offenders (except Richard Oliver, the younger, the master of the said vessel, and Richard Barrett, the younger, one of the owners thereof, and the persons who actually fired) who shall discover his accomplice or accomplices, or be the means of any one or more of them being apprehended and committed to prison for the said offence.

"And as a further encouragement, the Commissioners of His Majesty's Customs do hereby offer a Reward of Two Hundred Pounds, to any one of the said offenders (except as before excepted) or to any other person or persons who shall apprehend or cause to be apprehended, any one or more of them, the said Richard Oliver, the younger, Philip Libby, the younger, Thomas George, and Roger Toms, whose descriptions are hereinafter mentioned, which said reward will be paid by the Receiver-General of the Customs, upon the said persons, or either of them, being apprehended and committed to prison.

"By Order of the Commissioners, J.HUME, Secretary.

DESCRIPTIONS

"Richard Oliver, the younger, a dark complexion, long face, light brown curled short hair, about 6ft. high, about 26 years of age, rather thin, but very boney and walks very upright.

"Richard Barrett, the younger, a dark complexion, long thin face, black short straight hair, about 5ft. 6 ins. high, about 32 years of age, very thin, and rather stoops in his walk.

"Philip Libby, the younger, a dark complexion, round face, black short hair, about 6 ft. high, about 42 years of age, very stout, and rather stoops in his walk.

"William Swartman, the younger, a dark complexion, round face, long brown tied hair, about 5 ft. 4 ins. high, about 24 years of age, and of middling stature.

"Thomas George, a dark complexion, long thin face, and has a very wide mouth, short black hair, rather bald, about 5 ft. 4 ins. high, about 50 years of age, of a middling stature, and has lost part of the fore finger of one of his hands.

"Roger Toms, a very dark complexion, long face, short curled black hair, rather bald, about 5 ft. 5 or 6 ins. high, 45 years of age, middling stature, and has a rupture."

Toms was eventually discovered the following year on Guernsey where, according to Couch, the smugglers planned to ship him to America had he not been found by Government officers concealed in the hold of the vessel that was to convey him. Returned to Plymouth aboard the Revenue cutter *Swift* in April 1800, Toms was taken at once under military escort to Exeter gaol where Potter, the man he had denounced as Glinn's murderer, had been confined a year earlier.[9] While in prison he was again interviewed by Captain Bray, intent on discovering the whereabouts of the remaining members of the *Lottery* crew still at large.

The following month, the Collector of Customs at Plymouth wrote to the Board of Customs in London suggesting that the man who had harboured Toms on Guernsey could well have information which might lead to the arrest of the wanted men, thought to be in hiding on the island:

> 'We pray to observe that William Byfield who apprehended Toms appears to be a resident of Guernsey, in whose house Roger Toms remained three weeks and three days. It is therefore to be inferred that Byfield may have some knowledge of Oliver, Barrett and the other persons implicated in the murder of Humphry Glinn, against whom warrants have been granted, and be a useful person to assist the Bow Street officers in apprehending the offenders at Guernsey where they are supposed to be.'[10]

Tom Potter's Trial

With their principal witness now safely returned, the authorities wasted no time in bringing the case of the King against Thomas Potter, William Searle and Thomas Ventin for the murder of Humphry Glinn at the Old Bailey early in June. Two other prosection witnesses, Ambrose Bowden and Hugh Pearce, the *Hind*'s first officer at the time of the capture of the *Lottery* crew, set off from Plymouth by coach for London to attend the trial. From the outset, however, it was obvious that Bowden was unwell and by the time they had reached Exeter 'he was so ill,' according to Hugh Pearce, 'that he was unable to proceed.'[11]

The Cawsand Customs official did eventually manage to travel on as far as Egham in Surrey where, on June 9th, he lay 'dangerously ill' at the Kings Head Inn in the care of a local physician who certified that Bowden could not continue the journey to London 'without imminent danger to his life.' In the face of such medical evidence, the prosecution had little option but to ask once again for the trial to be postponed until such an important witness was able to attend and give evidence.

Was Bowden's strange and sudden illness genuine, or had he been got at? There is a curious entry among Job's papers relating to the *Lottery* trial, including one payment of £105 to Ambrose Bowden dated June 7th 1800, just two days before he was lying dangerously ill at Egham. What possible reason could Job have for giving such a large sum of money to one of the key prosecution witnesses in a trial involving Polperro smugglers? Another entry records that Job spent a further £112 on 'expence to and from London' in June that year, no doubt in connection with the trial.[12]

Whatever the reason for Bowden's indisposition, it did no more than delay the eventual trial for a further six months until December 10th 1800, nearly two years after Glinn's murder off Penlee Point, when the three former members of the *Lottery*'s crew appeared once more in the dock at the Old Bailey.

The most important evidence was given by Roger Toms who admitted being aboard the *Lottery* on the night in question. He named the prisoners Potter, Searle and Ventin as well as the men still sought in connection with Glinn's murder, Richard Oliver, Richard Barrett, William Swartman, Phillip Libby, Thomas George and a man called Irish Jack as having also been on board at the time.

The *Lottery* had left Polperro just before Christmas in 1798 for Guernsey where she had taken on a cargo of spirits and tobacco before sailing for Cawsand. At anchor off Penlee Point, Toms said he was below deck when the Revenue boat came up and he heard voices shouting 'Keep off!' and afterwards heard repeated 'It's a King's boat!' Several musket shots were fired from the *Lottery*, and some fired from the Revenue boat. Eventually orders were given to cut the cable.

After the *Lottery* had made her escape, Toms said in evidence he overheard her commander, Richard Oliver talking with Potter and Swartman. 'Thomas Potter said he had taken good level at the boat and had then fired his musket, and that he then looked and saw a man drop... Swartman said he had fired but not to hurt any person, only to frighten them.' Toms also testified that he had heard the *Lottery*'s commander give orders to Thomas Ventin, the ship's cook, to keep the pokers hot in the fire.[13]

Toms described in evidence how the *Lottery* arrived the following morning at Polperro where she delivered the remainder of her cargo before sailing for Guernsey. The following May she was taken by Captain Bray who commanded the Revenue cutter *Hind*. In cross-examination, Toms told how Captain Bray had put him and the rest of the Lottery crew in irons and how, for the first time, he gave this account to save his own life.

The main effort of the defence was aimed at discrediting Toms as a reliable witness. The prisoners' counsel, Mr Gurney, called several witnesses who all swore they knew Roger Toms to be a thief and a liar. These witnesses were closely cross-examined by the prosecuting counsel, intent on showing that they, as well as every other person living near the coast, were smugglers and therefore interested in protecting the prisoners. Summing up, Mr Justice Scott told the Old Bailey jury that everyone on board the *Lottery* at the time the shots that killed Humphry Glinn were fired was equally as guilty as the person who fired the fatal shot. The question was whether the prisoners were on board at the time, and that depended on the evidence of Roger Toms.

The jury, after retiring for nearly an hour, returned a verdict of guilty against Potter, but acquitted Searle and Ventin. The judge then pronounced the death sentence, addressing Potter at length and concluding with the macabre words:

'You will be conveyed to the place of execution on Friday next, and there hanged by the neck until you shall be dead, and your body afterwards given to be dissected and anatomised.'

Owing to the state of the tide on the Thames, however, the wretched Potter was kept at Newgate until the following week. On Thursday December

18th, he was taken the two miles to Execution Dock at Wapping. There, at the turn of the tide, Tom Potter met his end on the gallows set at low water mark in the customary manner reserved for those convicted of crime on the high seas.[14] A contemporary account says 'he conducted himself with great penitence and was attended by a Roman Catholic priest.'

There are a number of entries under the heading 'Lottery' among Job's papers that suggest he did what he could to help the unfortunate Potter. One item, dated May 15th 1799, the very day he was seized at home in Polperro by Captain Bray and the dragoons, says simply 'Gave Thos Potter £1.1.0", presumably to help him buy his own food; in those days prisoners had to pay for their own food or survive on the prison swill. Another refers to a sum of 16 guineas paid 'To the men in prison', no doubt intended for the 16 members of the *Lottery*'s crew confined aboard the *Hind* in Plymouth. In all, Job appears to have spent more than £700 in various payments for lawyers and other expences connected with the capture of the *Lottery*, including the mysterious payment of £105 to Ambrose Bowden just before he was due to testify against Potter in June 1800.[15] Did Bowden accept a bribe from Job, then feign illness, intending always to give evidence? The truth can only be guessed at. In 1814 the Custom House in London was burnt to the ground with most of its contents, and a few years later dozens of Job's account books were thrown onto a bonfire in Polperro after his death.

After Potter's execution, Roger Toms had good reason to fear for his life if he returned home to Polperro. According to Couch, 'even his children learned to detest him, and to this day his name is a term of reproach.' He was attached to Newgate prison as an assistant turnkey where he remained for the rest of his life. None of his family, wife or children ever wished to see him again.[16]

There was one other casualty of the *Lottery* episode. Humphry Glinn, a widower, left a ten-year-old son who, according to the Plymouth Collector of Customs 'appears destitute of friends and the means of support.' The Customs Board agreed to pay for the boy, who had 'a very great impediment in his speech and appears to be of tender constitution,' to attend a school at St Germans in Cornwall.[17]

Ambrose Bowden's courage in confronting the *Lottery* smugglers off Cawsand was rewarded with promotion to first officer of the Revenue cutter *Busy* stationed at Plymouth in 1800. For Gabriel Bray, however, the capture of the *Lottery* was to be the ultimate success in his long campaign against the smugglers. Not long after Potter's trial and execution ill health compelled him to relinquish his command of the *Hind* after a career spanning nearly thirty years in the King's service at sea.[18] In due course he joined the roll of Greenwich naval pensioners, having done more than anyone else to curb the smuggling trade at Polperro.

CHAPTER SIX: PREVENTIVE MEASURES

The hunt for the remaining members of the *Lottery* crew sought in connection with the murder of Humphry Glinn continued for many years afterwards. Detachments of cavalry would enter Polperro, searching boats in the harbour, walking up and down, muskets at the ready, looking everywhere for the missing men. Time after time the homes of the five wanted men would be surrounded at night by the dragoons, but on each occasion the fugitives were spirited away with the help of friends and neighbours. Every movement of the conspicuous red-coats was watched and word sent ahead to Polperro as soon as they left Plymouth. No one talked; no one gave the men away, despite the £200 reward which, to men and women earning a shilling a day, was a fortune. The community came to live in constant fear that the others would be taken and suffer the same fate as Tom Potter, dreading the sound of horses' hooves in the narrow cobbled streets of Polperro at the dead of night.

The *Lottery* incident, and Potter's subsequent trial and execution, proved to be a turning point in the determined struggle by the authorities to put an end to the smuggling trade at Polperro.

Instead of suffering the usual fate of vessels seized for smuggling at that time, and ordered to be sawn into three pieces or broken up and sold, the *Lottery* was taken into service at Plymouth by the Collector of Customs who reported she was 'very fit to cruise in the service, is in good condition and can soon be fitted out for sea...'[1]

The vessel evidently enjoyed some success against the very activity in which she had once been so actively engaged for, in September 1799, the Collector at Plymouth wrote to his counterpart at Looe:

'Mr Alexander Frazer, Commander of the *Lottery* temporary cruiser, having brought hither from Polperro the smuggling sloop

Assistance with 33 casks of spirits seized on board that vessel, we have to request that if the Officers of Polperro have any claim on the said vessel and goods, you will be pleased to transmit their pretentions to us...'[2]

The seizure of the *Assistance* followed an encounter at sea which ended with the *Lottery* pursuing both the *Assistance* and another smuggling vessel, the *Unity*, all the way into Polperro harbour. The commotion this caused can only be guessed at, but it certainly resulted in three local Revenue officers being dismissed from the service. A report by the Customs Board to the Controller at Looe refers to the 'improper and unjustifiable conduct' of the the three men, Nathanial Prynn, Charles Mallett and Samuel Sargeant. Prynn, a Riding Officer at Looe, and Mallett a boatman based at Polperro, were considered to be 'guilty of gross and criminal negligence' by witholding information from the *Lottery*'s commander and on suspicion of 'being in collusion with the smugglers.'[3]

A contemporary newspaper account of the incident reported from Plymouth in October 1799:

'Came in, the *Lottery*, revenue vessel, with the *Assistance*, smuggler, from Guernsey, with a cargo which the *Lottery* gallantly cut out in Polperro Bay.'[4]

By October, however, the *Lottery* had been declared 'unfit to go to sea' and of no further use to the Customs service. Having been officially condemned in the Court of Exchequer for smuggling, she was ordered to be broken up and sold. Gabriel Bray, as the seizing officer, was allowed the usual reward of ten shillings per ton from the proceeds, amounting to £47..10s for the 95 ton Lottery.[5]

The *Assistance* was not the only Polperro boat to be seized for smuggling by Revenue vessels at this time, as the following newspaper reports show:

Plymouth 16th June 1800
Arrived the *Spider* schooner with a smuggling lugger of Polperro called the *Expectation* with 900 ankers of spirits on board besides dry goods.

Fowey 30th May 1801
Hind Revenue cutter with Polperro boat laden with spirits.

Fowey 7th February 1803
Ranger with *Patience*, smuggling lugger of Polperro with 400 ankers of brandy and geneva.

Plymouth 28th May 1804
Came in the *Hunter* of 16 guns a ship from the eastwards with the *Brilliant* smuggling lugger, her prize of Polperro from Guernsey having on board 270 ankers of spirits.

Ashore, the Revenue officers often faced stubborn and, at times violent resistance. Even while the hunt for the *Lottery*'s crew was taking place in 1799, Christopher Childs, an Excise officer based at Looe was attacked by a gang of eight or nine smugglers at Pleaton between Polperro and Talland Bay. According to the Sherborne Mercury the gang 'rescued from him two ankers of spirit liquors which had just been seized there, and also abused him and very much ill-treated him.'[6] The Commissioners for Excise offered a reward of £20 for information leading to the conviction of Childs' assailants, but to no avail.

The Polperro smugglers suffered casualties of their own. At Talland church lies the headstone of Robert Mark, one of the crew of the Lottery at the time it was seized by the Revenue cutter *Hind* in 1799. Having served a term of imprisonment in connection with the incident, Mark was at the helm of a boat running into Polperro from a Revenue cutter when the cutter's crew opened fire, killing the helmsman on the spot. The inscription on his headstone reads:

ROBERT MARK
late of Polperro, who Unfortunately
was *shot at Sea* the 24th day of Jany.
in the year of our Lord GOD
1802, in the 40th Year of His AGE

Entrance to Polperro Harbour (1900)

Robert Mark's epitaph at Talland is similar to one in Lansallos churchyard recording the death of John Perry, Mariner, killed by a cannon ball, fired by a person unknown in 1779 when he was aged 24. Since England was at war with France at the time, it is more likely that Perry's death was the result of enemy action than that of the Revenue.

First Preventive Boat

Even before the *Lottery* episode Polperro had acquired an infamous reputation as a smuggling centre. The events of 1799 evidently persuaded the authorities that further measures were necessary to put a stop to it for, in January 1801, the Board of Customs in London wrote to the Collector at Looe announcing it 'thought it expedient to station a six-oared boat with a Sitter and six boatmen at Polperro' and that Mr Thomas Stap had been appointed as the Sitter at a salary of £50 per annum. Accordingly, six men were selected from the crews of the Revenue cutters Ranger and *Busy* who were willing to serve as boatmen and by April the first Custom House boat was stationed at Polperro. Cutlasses, muskets, pistols and ammunition were ordered to be issued to the crew.[7]

Given its reputation, it is hardly surprising that Polperro was chosen as one of the first sites for men of what later to be known as the Preventive Water Guard: 'For the suppressing of smuggling and outrage, the preservation of life and prosperity from shipwreck and of service for the Defence of the Nation.'

The arrival of the Preventive boat at Polperro must have caused considerable dismay among the smugglers as they watched its arrival at the quayside. Such was the local hostility shown to the seven men that not a single household would provide lodgings for them. Thomas Stap was compelled to ask 'that a seized vessel may be allowed him to moor in the harbour' because of the difficulty obtaining accommodation on shore.

The Collector at Plymouth reported that the only vessel there available for service at Polperro was the *John & Sarah*, seized for smuggling the previous year and in poor condition. In due course another former smuggling vessel called the Success was sent round from Fowey for Stap and his crew to live in.[8]

The *John & Sarah* was instead sold in July, the Plymouth Collector having satisfied himself that 'neither the owners or master have to our knowledge been convicted of smuggling.' His assessment of the *John and Sarah's* new master seems to have been misjudged, however, for on December 26th that same year he wrote again to the Board reporting that the *John and Sarah* had again been detained in Plymouth on suspicion of smuggling:

'This morning arrived here from sea the sloop *John and Sarah* of Polperro, Richard Mutton master, having sailed from Guernsey yesterday morning with spirits and tobacco. The master states that he was bound for Lisbon, but there does remain a doubt on our minds that his true destination was for Polperro or the neighbourhood of that famous smuggling town to which this vessel and her crew belong. We have had the vessel examined and find the cargo consists of small casks of about 7 gallons each, all fitted and prepared for the purpose of sinking, the said casks being all slung and thereby fastened at proper distances with sling yarn to a large hawser, having also a sufficient quantity of sinking stones with slings to them, suited for the purpose of keeping the casks down when sunk at a raft.'[9]

The practice of sinking kegs, or tubs as they were known, was used when the smugglers found it too risky to land their cargo because of the presence of riding officers or coastguards ashore. The kegs would be attached to a stout rope, as described by the Plymouth Collector, known as the 'sinking rope' which would be weighted with large stones. Once a suitable spot had been selected, kegs and rope would be cast off attached to an anchor to prevent them drifting. Well-secured in deep water, a cargo could lie for weeks without damage, though occasionally a fishing boat would land an unexpected catch. Job refers in a letter to one of the Guernsey merchants in 1797 to the misfortune of a Polperro smuggler who, 'after getting clear of all the cutters in the Channel and sinking his cargo, it was all taken up by a trawl boat who refused to deliver it to them and carried it off, giving them only a few ankers...'[10]

Method of Slinging Tubs

The tub-sling consisted of a piece of small left-handed rope (French),
secured round each end of the tub, so as to leave two ends, or "tails," of
equal length.   If the cargo was sunk, one only of these tails would be
used for fastening the tub to the sinking-rope, so that if, as was usually
the case, this tail was cut off in the hurry of "working" the crop,
there would still be one left.   The tub-carrier would then be able to
sling his pair of tubs by taking the tail from each tub over the shoulder
and securing it to the other tub,

Government Acts

With the end of what was then known as the War of the Revolution with France in 1802 came a brief respite during which time the armed smuggling vessels manned by reckless adventurers that roamed the Channel proved a source of considerable embarrassment to the Government. Measures were at once put in hand to curb their activities, but the Cornwall Gazette in February of that year greeted the news that a squadron of frigates was to be ordered to cruise off the Cornish coast against the smugglers with the suggestion that 'these frigates shall, at the end of twelve months, have seized as much spirits as will be equal to the regular consumption of their crews.'[11]

Such defiance was misplaced. A series of Government Acts intended to put a stop to the traffic in smuggled goods into Britain was approved by Parliament. Anyone found signalling from the shore to smugglers at sea was liable to a fine of £100, with rich rewards held out to informers. In 1805 an even more severe Act made it possible for any vessel found within 100 miles of the British coast with spirits, tobacco or tea in illegal packages on board liable to forfeiture. British anti-smuggling laws extended even to the Channel Islands, forbidding the movement of spirits, wine and tobacco to or from the islands in vessels of less than 100 tons (which included many of the Polperro fleet). The preventive powers given to Customs and Excise officers were extended to naval officers, allowing them to impress any detained smuggler.

The prospect of impressment into service aboard a naval man-of-war was something the Polperro smugglers feared more than imprisonment ashore. An earlier letter of Zephaniah Job's to one of the Guernsey merchants reported that 'the men are fearful to go out to sea for the late bustle with Press-gangs...'[12]

The Government hoped to make use of some of the experienced seamen found in smuggling craft by inviting convicted smugglers to serve aboard a King's ship. Naval life at that time was subject to harsh discipline however, and pressed seamen would often desert at the first opportunity.

Benjamin Rowett, who kept the New Inn on the pier at Polperro, had the misfortune to be impressed by a naval vessel while returning from a visit to the Channel Islands in August 1806. His wife, Mary, wrote to Carteret Priaulx, one of the Guernsey merchants with whom he dealt, on September 16th:

'I have to inform you that my husband Benjamin Rowett was taken coming from Alderney in a boat, and on Friday last sailed from Portsmouth for Guernsey in the *Sheldrake* sloop of war - have to request you the favour of using yourendeavours in getting him on shore...'[13]

No sooner had *HMS Sheldrake* returned to Portsmouth in October than Rowett deserted while on shore duty. A year later four Polperro men were among a number seized by a naval vessel, *HMS Recruit*; one of them, a 17-year-old youth named Robert Jeffery, was later marooned on a deserted Caribbean island by the *Recruit*'s captain.

Legislation designed to suppress smuggling along the coasts of Britain was also having an effect on the Guernsey merchants who supplied the smugglers. The Acts of 1805 and 1807 marked the end of the open smuggling trade in the Channel islands. Visiting Cornwall in April 1805 to recover outstanding debts from the smugglers and dealers he supplied with goods, Carteret Priaulx wrote to his brothers from Polperro that 'Pitt's infernal bill will I fear pass much too soon for us.'[14] Evidently concerned that yet more measures against smuggling would seriously affect his island's trade with the county, he added:

'This is a damn business for those who think and reflect; to ship and send accounts is nothing; to collect is the difficulty and at my age to be from my family is very unpleasant when a few years must carry me to my grave. I'm glad we shall not be long troubled with this damn business.'

Priaulx's stay in Polperro that year seems to have been a depressing occasion. 'Shortly after I came here to breakfast,' he wrote, 'I found the house mourning and doleful. Poor [William] Rowett.. died suddenly last night. Excess of drinking has killed him.' William, another member of the Rowett family whose smuggling and privateering exploits feature so much at this time, was the brother-in-law of Charles Guy, landlord of the Ship Inn at Polperro and one of Carteret Priaulx's agents.

Matters do not seem to have improved much when Carteret Priaulx's nephew, J.W.Gosselin, visited Cornwall early the following year and reported: 'Mr Johns has written me that it was useless for me to go at Polperro having nothing at present to pay but if he can raise any money will give it Mr Guy or send it here...'[15]

End of the Trade

The golden age of the 'Trade' as it was known in Polperro and elsewhere was coming to an end. Zephaniah Job, who had originally organised and managed the affairs of those engaged in smuggling, devoted his considerable energy to his many other business concerns. By the time the war with France had finally ended in 1815, and with it the end of privateering opportunities, Job's accumulated wealth included ownership of many farms and properties in the Polperro area as well as the harbour itself. Job's ownership of the harbour was a bad investment, however. On January 20th 1817, just four years after he bought it, Polperro was hit by a great storm of such severity that it destroyed almost everything in the harbour.

The West Briton on January 24th 1817 reported:

'At Polperro the ruin is dreadful; out of 45 fishing boats belonging to the place 30 have been dashed to atoms; most of those remaining are incapable of being repaired. Upwards of 60 families are deprived of bread. The pier is nearly destroyed and several dwellings and cellars washed away. Two seans[16] are totally lost and the greater part of the fish-salt in the town is washed away. Three new boats, all the timber and tools which were in the shipwright's yard have been carried away. The entire damage alone at Polperro is upwards of £6,000.'

Polperro Harbour (1888)

Job re-built the quays and repaired all the damage done to the harbour at enormous cost. In spite of this, he was still a comparatively wealthy man when he died at home in Polperro on January 31st 1822 at the age of 73. In his last illness he was attended by Dr Jonathan Couch, and the story of his death is that he ate a heavy meal at night and was found dead in bed the next morning. Curiously for a man who had always been so meticulous over the affairs of others, Job left no will. Cash totalling more than £1,442 was found at his house, enough to honour all the notes on his Polperro bank. After all expenses had been met his estate, much of which was sold by auction, was valued at £7,776.[17].

The 'Trade' continued for many years after Job's death, although it moved from Guernsey to Roscoff in Brittany. The government's measures to suppress it had proved largely successful and the Polperro Preventive boat was kept busy:

> West Briton, 15th May 1818
> 'On Saturday last, the Preventive boats at Polperro and Wrinkle took up a raft of contraband spirits near Looe Island, containing 106 ankers which they lodged in the excise warehouse at Looe.'

Occasionally such sunken cargo would be washed ashore. Over several weeks in 1825, a large quantity of smuggled liquor was found along the shore between Polperro and Fowey, some of which had been carried to Wheal Howell, a nearby tin mine. The Royal Cornwall Gazette reported on April 30th that a group of miners had drunk themselves into such a state of intoxication that they were only brought to the surface the following day with the utmost difficulty. The same evening a party of Preventive service men arrived with their officers to search the mine but found only one nearly empty keg of brandy!

The isolated nature of the coast below Lansallos made it ideal for the landing of smuggled goods. In March 1835, a gang of smugglers, several of whom were armed with clubs, was spotted making for Lantic Bay by two Coastguards patrolling the cliff top. According to an account in the Royal Cornwall Gazette, one of the Coastguards, Walter Harper, went to summon assistance while his companion remained hidden near Pencarrow Head. When Harper returned with four men, the Coastguards set off after the smugglers and, on confronting them, demanded the kegs they were carrying. The smugglers, armed with sticks and clubs, refused and a violent struggle ensued, resulting in one of the Coastguards being knocked unconscious but with five of the smugglers being taken prisoner. At the same time, a party of men from the Revenue cruiser *Fox* arrived on the scene and took the five prisoners in custody.

The *Fox* subsequently delivered 118 kegs of brandy seized that night, amounting to 484 gallons, to the Custom House at Fowey. The five prisoners stood trial at the Cornwall Assize, charged with 'assisting others in landing and carrying away prohibited goods, some being armed with offensive weapons'. The defence attempted to persuade Harper and his fellow officers to admit that the thick sticks carried by the smugglers were ordinary walking sticks carried by country people, but this they refused to do. Despite this the Cornish jury returned a verdict of not guilty (confirming the old saying: 'A Cornish jury will never convict a smuggler!'), adding that the sticks were not offensive weapons. As a result, the fortunate prisoners were discharged.

The episode had one other outcome. Commander Henry Shore in *Old Foye Days* records that, as a result of the affair at Lantic Bay, 'the last scrimmage of any importance between Coastguards and smugglers on the Cornish coast,' the authorities realised just how poorly guarded was the coast between Polperro and Fowey. A watch house was soon built overlooking Lantivet Bay and a detachment of Coastguards permanently stationed there. This effectively put a stop to much of the smuggling activity in the area.

With the suppression of the smuggling trade in Polperro came another change. Men whose families had sought to outwit and elude the Revenue cutters and Excise officers in earlier years now joined the newly-created Preventive Water Guard themselves. Others enlisted in the Royal Navy, often serving aboard the Revenue cutters that patrolled the coast of Cornwall in search of smugglers.

Polperro Street Scene (1907)

Reginald Langmaid, in all probability the son of John Langmaid whose trial at the Old Bailey in 1795 is referred to earlier, was admitted to the Custom House service at Plymouth in 1820 and is shown as Chief Boatman there in 1838. His son Thomas Stap Langmaid (grandson of The Polperro Preventive boat's first Sitter) also served aboard several Revenue cruisers from 1840.[18] By the mid 1850's more than fifty Polperro men were serving in the Navy or the Coastguard.

As Couch himself records, 'the contraband trade became too dangerous to be profitable, antipathies wore out, the Preventive men made themselves agreeable to the people they had come amongst.' Polperro had brought up a succession of hardy and skilful sailors 'some of whom have been engaged in our most distinguished naval engagements.' It became the ambition of many men and boys there to join the very services their fathers and grandfathers hated and feared. Smuggling was never completely eradicated from the area, but it never again enjoyed the communal support it had in Polperro during Zephaniah Job's lifetime.

APPENDIX: POLPERRO'S SMUGGLING CHRONOLOGY

1778	February 6	England declares war with France.
1780	April 17	War with Spain.
	December 21	War with Holland.
1781	July 11	*Swallow* captures *Le Rusee.*
	July 18	*Harlequin* seizes *Swallow.*
1782	November 30	War with American colonies ends.
1783	January 20	War with France and Spain ends.
	April 19	*HMS Beaver* seizes *Swallow.*
1786	May	Zephaniah Job appointed steward to Sir Harry Trelawny.
1793	February 1	France declares war on England.
1794	March 5	Revenue officers raid on Richard Rowett's cellar at Polperro.
1795	October 28	Trial of John Langmaid at Old Bailey.
1798	April 28	Captain Gabriel Bray attempts seizure of contraband at Polperro.
	August	*Sedwell* condemned for smuggling.
	December 26	*Lottery* surprised at Cawsand; Humphry Glinn killed.
1799	May 13	Revenue cutter *Hind* captures *Lottery.*
	May 15	Tom Potter seized at Polperro.

	June 14	Roger Toms abducted at Polruan.
	July 23	Christopher Childs, Excise Officer at Looe, attacked near Polperro.
	September 19	*Lottery*, in Revenue service, seizes *Assistance* at Polperro.
	December 20	Trial of Potter, Searle and Ventin at Old Bailey postponed.
1800	April	Roger Toms recaptured at Guernsey.
	June 9	Ambrose Bowden taken ill at Egham; *Lottery* trial again postponed.
	December 10	Trial of Potter, Searle and Ventin at Old Bailey.
	December 18	Tom Potter executed.
1801	April	First Preventive Boat stationed at Polperro.
1802	January 24	Robert Mark killed at sea (buried at Talland).
	March 27	Peace with France.
1803	April 29	War declared between England and France.
1804	May	*Brilliant* seized by *HMS Hunter* for smuggling.
1815	June 18	War against Bonaparte ends.
1817	January 20	Storm wrecks Polperro harbour.
1822	January 31	Zephaniah Job dies at Polperro.

BIOGRAPHICAL NOTES

Zephaniah Job (1749-1822) 'The Smugglers' Banker'. Came to Polperro from St Agnes (c 1770). Schoolmaster, later steward to Sir Harry Trelawny (1786), merchant, agent and business advisor to Polperro smugglers.

Sir Harry Trelawny (1756-1834) 7th baronet. Married Anne (1778). Four sons, two daughters. Magistrate and cleric, ordained first Non-Conformist minister, then Anglican (1781). Later became a Catholic, finally ordained in Rome (1830).

THE SMUGGLERS:

John Quiller (1741-1804) Married Jane Libby (1763). Father of Richard (b. 1763), William (b 1765) and John (b 1771). Owner of *Three Brothers, Swallow, Brilliant* and *Lively.*

Richard Quiller (1763-1796) Brother of William (b 1765) and John (b 1771). Married Mary Toms (1784). Owner of *Richard and Mary* and commander of *Lively.*

William Quiller (1765-1815) Brother of Richard (b 1763) and John (b 1771). Married Phillipa Toms (1785).

Richard Rowett (1770-1848) Married Phillis Johns (1790). Eldest son of Richard (1746-1796). Commander of *Unity.*

Benjamin Rowett (1764-?) Cousin of Richard (b 1770). Married Mary Johns (1794). Innkeeper of New Inn Polperro.

William Johns (1742-1802) Married Phillipa Libby (1766). Father of Phillis (m Richard Rowett) and Mary (m Benjamin Rowett). Owner of *Swallow* and *Brilliant.*

John Langmaid (1756-1829) Married Mary Libby (1778). Father of Reginald (b 1800).

Richard Oliver (1772-1830) Owner and commander of *Lottery* (1799).

John Clements Married Jane Quiller (1791). Owner of schooner *Polperro* (1806).

Thomas Potter (1774-1800) Married Mary Libby (1797) Lottery crewman, convicted and executed for murder of Humphry Glinn.

Roger Toms (1759-?) Brother of Mary (m Richard Quiller). Married Martha Mark (1783). *Lottery* crewman seized 1799.

THE REVENUE MEN:

Gabriel Bray (1750-1823) Commissioned Lieutenant in Royal Navy (1773). Commander of Revenue cutter Hind (1793-1800)

Ambrose Bowden (1750-?) Sitter of Custom House boat at Cawsand at the time of the Lottery incident (1798). Mate of Revenue cutter Busy (1800).

Thomas Pinsent Custom House officer stationed at Polperro from 1766. Resigned 1796. Died 1796.

CREW OF POLPERRO PREVENTIVE BOAT 1801:

Thomas Stap (Sitter)
William Churchill
Thomas Staton
Thomas Wakeham
Thomas Botting
John Hoyle
Richard Widger

THE GUERNSEY MERCHANTS:

Jersey and De Lisle (Peter De Lisle & Sons)
De Carteret & Co. (Carteret Priaulx)
Nicholas Maingy & Brothers
John Lukis

THE LONDON AGENTS:

William De Jersey
Perchard & Brock (Perchard Brock & LeMesurier)
Bonamy Dobree & Co.

Polperro Boats (1908)

POLPERRO BOATS

BRILLIANT   Lugger; 120 tons; crew 60;
                            12 carriage guns, 6 swivels.
                            Owners included John Quiller (1784),
                            William Johns (1786)
                            Seized for smuggling May 1804

LIVELY   Sloop; 111 tons; crew 40;
                            19 carriage guns, 4 swivels.
                            Owners included John Quiller (1793),
                            Nicholas Maingy (1796)

LOTTERY   Cutter; 94 tons; crew 15.
                            Seized for smuggling May 1799

RICHARD AND MARY Brig
                            Owned by Richard Quiller (1796)

SEDWELL   Cutter; 86 tons; crew 50;
                            10 carriage guns, 12 swivels.
                            Owners included Zephaniah Job (1793)
                            Seized for smuggling 1798

SWALLOW   Lugger; 80 tons; crew 20
                            12 swivel guns
                            Owners included John Quiller (1780),
                            William Johns (1780), Zephaniah Job.
                            Seized for smuggling April 1783.

THREE BROTHERS   Shallop.
                            Owners included John Quiller (1785),
                            Zephaniah Job (1795).

UNITY   Lugger; 102 tons; crew 40;
                            10 carriage guns, 2 swivels.
                            Owners included Richard Rowett.

BIBLIOGRAPHY

Primary Sources
Zephaniah Job Records
    Royal Institution of Cornwall
        ZJ11a Letter-book 1785-1789
        ZJ32   Letter-book 1795-1798
        ZJ7   General accounts day-book 1778-1787
Carteret Priaulx Papers
    Priaulx Library, Guernsey
Admiralty Records
    Public Record Office
        ADM1 Captains Letters 1782-1784
        ADM1 Revenue Cruiser Hind 1802
        ADM7 Ships Seized while Smuggling 1783-1793
        CUST21 Register of Seizures
        CUST31 Board to Collectors, Western Ports
        CUST66 Letter-books, Plymouth Collector
        HCA1 Trial of Thomas Potter 1799-1800
        HCA32 Prize Papers
        KB11/32 Rowett etc. 1798 case
Newspaper Reports
    British Newspaper Library
        The Times 1795-1801
        Sherborne & Yeovil Mercury 1780-1800
        Royal Cornwall Gazette 1802-1852
        West Briton 1810-1840

Secondary Sources
Cox, Gregory Stevens *Guernsey & the French Revolution*, Guille-Alles Library 1989
Couch, Jonathan *History of Polperro* W.Lake Truro 1871
De Burlet, Sheila *Portrait Of Polperro* Rooster 1977
Harper, Charles G. *The Smugglers* Chapman & Hall 1909
Noall, Cyril *Smuggling In Cornwall* D.Bradford Barton Ltd 1971

Perrycoste, Frank H. *Gleanings from the Records of Zephaniah Job of Polperro* 1930

Raban, Canon Peter *Clandestine Trade in the Mid-Eighteenth Century* La Societe Guernesaise 1987

Shore, Commander Henry N. Smuggling Days and Smuggling Ways Cassell & Co. 1892

Shore, Commander Henry N. *Old Foye Days* 1907

White, Margaret *The Carteret Priaulx Papers*

Further Reading

Halliday F.E. *A History of Cornwall* Duckworth 1959

Hamilton Jenkin, A.K. *Cornwall and its People* J.M.Dent 1945

Hippisley Coxe, Anthony D. *A Book About Smuggling in the West Country 1700-1850* Tabb House 1984

Johnston, Peter *A Short History of Guernsey* Guernsey Press 1976

Smith, Graham *King's Cutters The Revenue Service and the War Against Smuggling* Conway Maritime Press 1983

Ward-Jackson C.H. *Ships and Shipbuilders of a Westcountry Seaport*: Fowey 1786-1939 Twelveheads Press 1986

Webb, William *Coastgaurd!* An Official History of HM Coastguard HMSO 1976

Wilson, Joy *East Cornwall in the Olden Days* Bossiney Books 1988

Vivian, John *Tales of the Cornish Smugglers* Tor Mark Press

NOTES AND REFERENCES

Chapter 1 FREE-TRADERS AND FORTUNE

1   Jonathan Couch *History of Polperro*, edited by Thomas Quiller Couch 1871 p.100. Couch gives the 1801 Census returns for the two parishes of Lansallos and Talland within which Polperro lies, adding 'Polperro may be set down as having a population little short of a thousand'

2   Zephaniah Job letter to John Owen Parr, November 11 1795, requesting insurance on cargo of 450 hogsheads of pilchards aboard the *Richard and Mary* in Fowey, bound for Italy: ZJ32 Royal Institution of Cornwall. Couch's *History* p.108 gives the contents of a hogshead as 3,000 fish

3   F.E.Halliday, *A History of Cornwall* 1959 p.263

4   *Chambers's Encyclopaedia* 1901 Vol.IX p.121

5   Charles G. Harper, *The Smugglers* 1909 p.184

6   Journal of Federation of Old Cornwall Societies, October 1925, p.6

7   John Wesley at St Ives, 1753: Journals (ed. N. Curnock) 1909-16

8   Sheila de Burlet, *Portrait of Polperro* 1977, p.19

9   Frank H. Perrycoste, *Gleanings from the Records of Zephaniah Job of Polperro* 1930, p.1 and 130.

10   Canon Peter Raban, *Clandestine Trade in the Mid-Eighteenth Century* 1987, p.321

11   Gregory Stevens Cox, *Guernsey & the French Revolution*, Guille-Alles Library 1989

12   Job to Jersey and De Lisle, January 20 1788: ZJ11a

13   Job to De Carteret & Co., September 23 1788: ZJ11a

14   Ibid, January 17 1789

15   Job to Carteret Priaulx, June 26 1795: ZJ32

16   Job to John Lukis, May 10 1796: ZJ32

17   Perrycoste, *Gleanings.*. p.137

18   Job to Nicholas Maingy, June 16 1787: ZJ11a

19   Minchinton, *Piracy and Privateering*, p.300

20   Job Letter-book, September 26 1797: ZJ32

21   Job Letter-book, November 1786: ZJ11a

22   Job to Le Mesurier, September 25 1786: ZJ11a

23   Perrycoste, *Gleanings.*. p.148

24   Job to Messrs Lessier & Wood, agents for the *Brilliant*, May 18 1795: ZJ32

25   A.K.Hamilton Jenkin, *Cornish Seafarers* 1932 p.32

Chapter 2 THE SMUGGLERS' BANKER

1   John Wesley's Journal Vol IV p.527 (Sep.16 1768)

2   Couch *History of Polperro* 1871 p.89

3   John Clements' exercise book ZJ6 R.I.C.

4   Job to J.P.Carpenter, July 15 1796: ZJ32

5   Job to Sir Harry Trelawny, January 8 1786: ZJ11a

6   Perrycoste, *Gleanings.*. p.30

7   Ibid, p.142

8   Ibid, p.154

9   Private memoirs of Jonathan Couch, f.20, R.I.C.

10   Perrycoste, *Gleanings.*. p.147

11 HCA32/291/1, PRO

12 Job to Peter Perchard, May 31 1785: ZJ11a

13 Ibid, June 16 1785

14 Job refers to Richard Quiller's death in a letter to Nicholas Maingy in December 1796: ZJ32

15 Thomas Quiller Couch in the introduction to his father's *History of Polperro*, p.9

16 Job to John Lukis, December 5 1795: ZJ32

17 Perrycoste, p.134

18 Job to Peter De Lisle, January 20 1789: ZJ11a

19 Job to Bonamy Dobree & Co., February 6 1789: ZJ11a

20 Perrycoste, p.141

21 Job to Peter De Lisle & Sons, May 24 1796: ZJ32

22 Job letter dated November 1 1796, no addressee given but reference to 'your and Mrs Carpenters good company' suggests it was John Phillipps Carpenter: ZJ32

Chapter 3 THE SWALLOW'S TALE

1 Job Ledger (1778-1786): ZJ7 R.I.C.

2 HCA32/444, PRO

3 HCA32/458, PRO

4 Job to Fairbank, February 20 1787: ZJ11a

5 Job to Thomas Bowerbank, August 15 1788: ZJ11a

6 ADM1/2307, PRO

7 Ibid

8   Ibid

9   E159/238, PRO

10   ADM1/2307

11   Ibid

12   Job Ledger (1778-1786): ZJ7

13   ADM1/2307

Chapter 4 POLPERRO AND THE REVENUE MEN

1   Pinsent said in evidence at the trial of John Langmaid in October 1795 that he
had been a Custom House Officer at Polperro for 29 years: Old Bailey Sessions papers
Vol. 72 pt.II

2   Couch, *History of Polperro* p.83. Cellars in Polperro were usually at ground
floor level for curing pilchards

3   Old Bailey Sessions papers, Vol. 72 pt.II, p.1325

4   Ibid

5   Job to J.P.Carpenter, November 1795: ZJ32

6   Job to Peter De Lisle & Sons, March 10 1797: ZJ32

7   Job to James Tippett, June 27 1797: ZJ32

8   Job to Nicholas Maingy & Bros., November 22 1797: ZJ32

9   Ibid, September 14 1797

10   Job to John Lukis, August 1 1797: ZJ32

11   KB32/2, PRO

12   Ibid

13   KB11/60, PRO

Chapter 5 THE LOTTERY'S LAST CHANCE

1   HCA1/25/341, PRO

2   Evidence of Roger Toms: hca1/85/193, PRO

3   Couch, History of Polperro, p.86

4   HCA1/25

5   Plymouth Collector of Customs to Board, May 18 1799: CUST66/1, PRO

6   HCA1/85/283

7   HCA1/85/282

8   Plymouth Collector of Customs to Board, July 20 1799: CUST66/1

9   Abid, April 22 1800

10   Ibid, May 2 1800

11   HCA1/25/359

12   Loose slip of paper inserted in Thomas Quiller Couch's unpublished MS at the Royal Institution of Cornwall library, Truro, headed: 1799 Lottery 11/1/99 (possibly in Job's handwriting)

13   HCA1/85/193

14   HCA1/85/193. Details of Execution Dock courtesy of the National Maritime Museum

15   See Note 11

16   Couch, *History of Polperro*, p.88

17   Plymouth Collector of Customs to Board, May 18 1799: CUST66/1

18   There are several references to Bray's ill health among correspondence from the Customs Board to Collectors at Western Ports (CUST31/7 etc). The Navy List for 1800

lists Bray as Lieutenant but not serving on any vessel. The 1811 Navy List has him as a Greenwich pensioner and incapable of service. He died on December 6 1823

Chapter 6 PREVENTIVE MEASURES

1   Plymouth Collector of Customs to Board, June 29 1799: CUST66/1

2   Plymouth Collector of Customs to Collector, Looe, September 23 1799: CUST66/1

3   Customs Board to Looe Collector, January 3 1801: CUST31/7

4   I am grateful to Sheila de Burlet for permission to use this and other references from her unpublished MS of Polperro's history

5   Plymouth Collector to Board, March 22 1800: CUST66/1

6   Sherborne Mercury, October 7 1799

7   Customs Board to Looe Collector, January 17 1801

8   Ibid, May 5 1801

9   Plymouth Collector to Board, December 26 1801

10   Job to John Lukis, August 1 1797: ZJ32

11   Royal Cornwall Gazette, February 13 1802

12   Job to Nicholas Maingy, November 1 1787: ZJ11a

13   Carteret Priaulx papers, Guernsey. I am indebted to James Derriman for this extract

14   Carteret Priaulx to brothers, April 22 1805: C.P.P. Guernsey

15   J.W. Gosselin to Carteret Priaulx & Co., January 17 1806: C.P.P.

16   Seans or seins were a type of fishing boat used for catching pilchards. According to Couch in his *History of Polperro* (p105), 'the crew of a sean consists of eighteen men and, commonly, a boy'.

17   Perrycoste, *Gleanings..* p.162-163. According to Perrycoste, Job was burried at Lansallos

18   I am grateful to Mark Faulknall for details of the Langmaid family

INDEX

REVIEWS of Polperro's Smuggling Story:

" The author deserves our congratulations for bringing Polperro and its smuggling story so vividly to the printed page."
Mariners' Mirror

"It is doubtful whether the best of novelists could have developed a better plot than Jeremy Johns' story of the hard men who made a good living from their frightening, dangerous trade. All the elements of a good story are there, made the more vital by being true."
Cornish World

"An ideal purchase for summer visitors and for any lover of Cornwall and the country's chequered history."
Sunday Independent

"Excellent... A well researched book that increases our knowledge of those hard times."
Cornwall Family History Society Journal

"I can heartily recommend this book to like-minded sea rovers."
Tony Pawlyn, *South West Soundings*

"Fascinating and entertaining... an essential addition to the bookcase."
Cornish Times

"A must for anyone intrigued by the illegal pursuits of some Cornish folk around the 18th C."
Cornish Forefathers Society Journal